I0832781

MILLER'S

NEW YORK AS IT IS;

OR

STRANGER'S GUIDE-BOOK

TO THE CITIES OF

NEW YORK, BROOKLYN

AND ADJACENT PLACES:

COMPRISING NOTICES OF

EVERY OBJECT OF INTEREST TO STRANGERS;

INCLUDING

PUBLIC BUILDINGS, CHURCHES, HOTELS, PLACES OF AMUSEMENT, LITERARY INSTITUTIONS, ETC.

With Map and numerous Illustrations.

NEW YORK:
JAMES MILLER, 522 BROADWAY.
1866.

CONTENTS.

PAGE.

Historical Localities.......... 5
Historic Retrospect.......... 13
General View.......... 20
New York as it is.......... 23
Parks and Public Squares.......... 27
Public Buildings.......... 35
Benevolent Institutions.......... 39
Literary and Scientific Institutions.......... 48
Theological Institutions.......... 58
New York Press.......... 60
Places of Amusement.......... 63
Carmen.......... 65
Hotels.......... 63
Churches of New York.......... 71
Elegant Private Residences.......... 80
Notable Stores, &c.......... 82
Banks.......... 86
Savings Banks.......... 88
Public Works.......... 89
Clipper Ships, Packets, &c.......... 92
Forts and Fortifications.......... 92
Principal Restaurants and Saloons.......... 93
Principal Hotels.......... 94
New York Markets.......... 94
Ocean Steamships.......... 95
Telegraph Lines.......... 98
Foreign Consuls.......... 96
Omnibuses and Rail Cars.......... 99
Railroads.......... 102
The Ferries.......... 104
Expresses and depots.......... 105
List of Piers.......... 106
The City of Brooklyn.......... 107
Brooklyn Hotels.......... 112
——— Public Institutions.......... 112
Greenwood Cemetery.......... 113
Churches of Brooklyn.......... 115
Brooklyn City Railroads.......... 117
Pleasure Excursions.......... 118
The Environs of the City.......... 120
Distances in the City.......... 122
The Hudson River.......... 123
Supplemental Hints.......... 128
Metropolitan Police.......... 133

LIST OF ILLUSTRATIONS.

	PAGE
View of Broadway from Dr. Chapin's Church	
do. do. do. Exchange Place	
The City Hall	35
Custom House	36
Sub-Treasury	37
Arsenal of New York	38
Halls of Justice, or the "Tombs"	39
New York Hospital	41
——— Institution for the Blind	44
Odd Fellows' Hall	46
The Cooper Union	49
New York University	55
Bible House	57
Episcopal Theological Seminary	58
Metropolitan Hotel	65
Astor House	66
St. Nicholas Hotel	67
Prescott House	68
Clarendon Hotel	69
St. Denis Hotel	70
Fifth Avenue Hotel	71
Church of the Puritans	74
St. Patrick's Cathedral	75
First Presbyterian Church	76
Calvary Church	79
Dr. Alexander's Church	80
Tiffany's Store	83
Bank of the Republic	86
Bowery Savings Bank	88
Croton Reservoir	89
High Bridge	90

NEW YORK AS IT WAS.

HISTORICAL LOCALITIES.

The denizens of New York are such utilitarians that they have sacrificed to the shrine of Mammon almost every relic of the olden time. The feeling of veneration for the past, so characteristic of the cities of the Old World, is lamentably deficient among the people of the New. Still, as there are some who may take an interest in knowing even the sites of memorable historic places of the city, we will briefly refer to some of them. Few, we presume, are not patriotic enough to gaze with interest as they pass through Franklin Square, on the site of the old town mansion of Washington, which stood at the northeast angle of Franklin Square and Pearl street; or tread the sod of Fort Greene, Brooklyn, that battle-ground of the Martyrs of Liberty.

Taking the Battery as a starting-point, the first object of historic interest we encounter, is the old *Kennedy House*, No. 1 Broadway. During the war of independence, it was successively the residence of Lord Cornwallis, Gen. Clinton, Lord Howe, and Gen. Washington. This house was erected in 1760, by Hon. Capt. Kennedy, who returned to England prior to the Revolution. It subsequently came into the possession of his youngest son, from whom it ultimately passed into that of the late Nathaniel Prime. Talleyrand passed some time under its roof.

From this house anxious eyes watched the destruction of the statue of George III., in the Bowling Green; and a few years afterwards, other eyes saw, from its windows, the last soldiers of that king passing forever from our shores. Still later, others looked sadly on the funeral of Fulton, who died in a house which had been built in what was once the garden.

Here Arnold concerted his treasonable project with André at the Clinton's—his head-quarters at the time. Arnold also occupied more frequently the third house from the Battery, in Broadway. Arnold is said to have had a sentinel at his door. When his traitorous character had become known, he used to be saluted in the streets by the epithet of "the traitor-general." He was guarded by an escort from Sir Henry Clinton. Gen. Gage's head-quarters, in 1765, was the small low building since known as the Atlantic Garden.

The Bowling Green was originally inclosed, in 1732, "with walks therein for the beauty and ornament of said street, as well as for the sports and delight of the inhabitants of the citie."

In 1697, it was resolved "that the lights be hung out in the darke time of the moon within this citty, and for the use of the inhabitants; and that every 7th house doe hang out a lanthorn and a candle in it," &c.

The site of the old Government house is now occupied by a range of dwelling-houses, at the south side of the inclosure, called the Bowling Green. It was subsequently used as the Custom House (from 1790 to 1815), when it was taken down. Earlier recollections even belong to this location; here the Dutch and English forts were erected. At the corner of Wall and William streets, now the Bank of New York, once stood the statue of William Pitt. The old Stadt Huys stood at Coenties Slip. On the site of the present U. S. Treasury, was situated the Town Hall, or "Congress Hall," which included also the Law Courts and Prison. In front of this building were the stocks, a pillory, and a whipping-post. This edifice was subsequently converted into a hall of legislature.

It was in its gallery, on Wall street, in April, 1789, that Gen. Washington was inaugurated *the first Presi-*

dent of the United States. This important public ceremony, the oath of office, took place in the *open gallery* in front of the Senate Chamber, in the view of an immense concourse of citizens. There stood Washington, invested with a suit of dark silk velvet, of the old cut, steel-hilted small-sword by his side, hair in bag and full powdered, in black silk hose, and shoes with silver buckles, as he took the oath of office, to Chancellor Livingston. Dr. Duer thus describes the scene of the inauguration:

"This auspicious ceremony took place under the portico of Federal Hall, upon the balcony in front of the Senate Chamber, in the immediate presence of both Houses of Congress, and in full view of the crowds that thronged the adjacent streets. The oath was administered by Chancellor Livingston, and when the illustrious chief had kissed the book, the Chancellor, with a loud voice, proclaimed, "Long live George Washington, President of the United States." Never shall I forget the thrilling effect of the thundering cheers which burst forth, as from one voice, peal after peal from the assembled multitude. Nor was it the voices alone of the people that responded to the announcement, their *hearts* beat in unison with the echoes resounding through the distant streets; and many a tear stole down the rugged cheeks of the hardiest of the spectators, as well I noted from my station in an upper window of the neighboring house of Col. Hamilton."

Washington's farewell interview with his officers took place at France's Tavern, corner of Pearl and Broad streets.

New York is noted for its pageants and processions. That on the occasion of the last visit of Gen. Lafayette, presented the most imposing spectacle of its time.

In ancient times boats were used to convey passengers across Pearl street. Canal and Cliff streets derive their names from a like circumstance. The Old Dutch records show that the outskirts of the town were divided into farms—called "Bouwerys;" From this fact the Bowery derived its name.

The hills were sometimes precipitous, as from Beekman's and Peck's hills, and in the neighborhood of Pearl, Beekman, and Ferry streets, and from the Middle Dutch Church, in Nassau street, down to Maiden lane; and sometimes gradually sloping, as on either hills along the line of the water, coursing through Maiden lane.

When Hamilton acted as Secretary of the Treasury, he wrote the "Federalist," at a house in Wall street, between Broad and William streets, its site being now occupied by the Mechanics' Bank. His last residence was the Grange, at Bloomingdale. He lived also for some time at Bayard House on the banks of the North River. His hapless duel with Burr, near Weehawken, is pointed out to visitors,—a stone marks the spot where Hamilton fell.

Leisler and Milbourne, the proto-martyrs of popular liberty in America, met with a sanguinary death, May 16th, 1691, on the verge of Beekman's swamp, near the spot where Tammany Hall now stands.

Where Catharine street now stands, was the spot where the stamps were burnt, at the dead of night, by citizens, in the year 1776.

Benjamin Franklin, while residing in New York, used as an observatory for experimenting on electricity, the steeple of the old Dutch Church,—now the Post-Office, in Nassau street. Who will not gaze with interest at this starting-point of that luminous train which now encircles the globe, and by which we communicate in letters of light, with our antipodes, almost with the celerity of thought.

The old City Hotel, in Broadway, the site of which is now occupied by a row of brown stone buildings, was for a long time the most notable edifice of the kind in the city. Here Washington, with his suite, attended the brilliant assemblies of his days.

A still more interesting relic of the past, was the old

Sugar-House Prison, which, till within a very few years, stood in Liberty street, adjacent to the Dutch Church, now the Post-Office. It was founded in 1689, and occupied as a sugar-refining factory, till 1777, when Lord Howe converted it into a place of confinement for American prisoners. Here is a sketch of it.

The old Walton House, in Pearl street (No. 326), was one of the memorabilia of New York city. This celebrated mansion was erected, in 1754, by Walton, a wealthy English merchant. It continued in possession of the family during the Revolutionary war, and was the scene of great splendor and festivity.

Washington's city mansion stood at the junction of Main and Pearl streets—the northern angle of Franklin Square. Here the General was accustomed to hold state levees.

The Old Brewery, at the Five Points, recently taken down, is deserving of some notice. Its purlieus were those of wretchedness and crime; they have been fitly described as "an exhibition of poverty without a parallel—a scene of degradation too appalling to be believed, and too shocking to be disclosed, where you find crime without punishment,—disgrace without shame,—sin without compunction,—and death without hope."

During the past few years, the attention of the benevolent has been attracted to this locality, and a missionary station has been erected there, under the direction of Mr. Pease. The entire cost of the establishment has been estimated at over $80,000.

The old Methodist Church in John street, nearly facing Dutch street, is an object of antiquarian interest. In William street, about midway between John and Fulton streets, stands a range of modern houses, about the centre of which was the birth-place of Washington Irving.

Old Governor Stuyvesant's house, a fine view of which is annexed, stood upon his "Bowerie Farm," a little to the south of St. Mark's Church, between the Second and Third Avenues. A pear-tree, imported

SUB-TREASURY.

from Holland in 1647, by Stuyvesant, and planted in his garden, yet flourishes on the corner of Thirteenth street and Third Avenue, the only *living* relic which preserves the memory of the renowned Dutch Govnor. This patriarchal tree is two hundred and twelve years old.

We present the reader with a *fac-simile* of Governor Stuyvesant's seal.

He lived eighteen years after the change in the government, and at his death was buried in his vault within the chapel. Over his remains was placed a slab (which may yet be seen in the eastern wall of St. Mark's), with the following inscription: "In this vault lies buried Petrus Stuyvesant, late Captain General and Commander-in-Chief of Amsterdam, in New Netherlands, now called New York, and the Dutch West India Islands. Died in August, A. D., 1682, aged eighty years."

At the corner of Charlton and Varick streets stood a wooden building, formerly of considerable celebrity, known as the "Richmond Hill House." It has had many distinguished occupants, having been successively the residence of General Washington, John Adams, and Aaron Burr. It has been the scene of great festivities. Baron Steuben, Chancellor Livingston, and numerous

other notable men of their times, having met within its walls.

Aaron Burr once lived at the corner of Cedar and Nassau streets, and, after he held the office of Vice-President, at the corner of Pine and Nassau.

Cobbett kept his seed store at 62 Fulton street. His farm was at Hempstead, Long Island.

Grant Thorburn's celebrated seed store, which was one of the notable objects of the city, in its time, was in Liberty street, between Nassau and Broadway, and occupied as large a space as the present establishment in John street. His store was previously used for a Quaker meeting-house, the first that that society had erected in the city.

The brick meeting-house, built in 1764, in Beekman

street, near Nassau street, then standing on open fields, was the place where Whitefield preached.

On the site of the present Metropolitan Hotel, once lived the diplomatist—Talleyrand, when ambassador to the United States. He published a small tract on America, once much read; he it was who affirmed that the greatest sight he had ever beheld in this country, was Hamilton, with his pile of books under his arm, proceeding to the court-room in the old City Hall, in order to expound the law.

James Rivington, from London, opened a bookstore in 1761, near the foot of Wall street, from which his "Royal Gazetteer" was published in April, 1773.

Gaine's "New York Mercury," in Hanover Square, was established in 1752; Holt's "New York Journal," in Dock (Pearl) street, near Wall, commenced in 1776; and Anderson's "Constitutional Gazette," a very small sheet, was published for a few months in 1775, at Beekman's Slip.

Gaine kept a bookstore under the sign of the Bible and Crown, at Hanover Square, for forty years. Among the early publishers and booksellers, may be named, Evert Duyckinck, who lived at the corner of Pearl street and Old Slip; and Isaac Collins, George A. Hopkins, Samuel Campbell, and T. & J. Swords.

William Barlas, of Maiden Lane, was himself an excellent scholar. He published classical books. He was the friend and correspondent of Newton—Cowper's friend.

HISTORICAL RETROSPECT.

In the year 1607, the memorable year in which forty-seven learned men began the English version of the Bible, Henry Hudson sailed in search of a northeast passage to India. For two seasons he strove in vain to penetrate the ice barriers, and then turned homeward. His patrons abandoned their enterprise, and Hudson went over to Holland and entered the service of the Dutch East India Company, whose fleets then agitated the waters of almost every sea.

On the 3d of September, 1609, the intrepid navigator first entered the Bay of New York. Here commence the acknowledged chronicles of European civilization on these shores of the newly-discovered continent, over which, till then, the wild Indian had held undisputed sway. According to Scandinavian records, it is affirmed, the Norsemen visited our shores even prior to the discovery of the continent by the famed Genoese.

Among those supposed early navigators, was Prince Madoc; and Verrazani, who, in the year 1514, is believed to have anchored in these waters, and explored the coast of what was then known as part of ancient Vinland. We shall take a cursory glance at the leading events which have been handed down to us, since they will serve to illustrate the progressive advancement of the civilized, over the savage forms of life, of which this memorable island has been the theatre.

Although Hudson has not recorded, in his diary, his landing in the harbor of New York, we possess a tradition of the event, by Heckewelder, the Indian historian. He describes the natives as greatly perplexed and terrified when they beheld the approach of the strange object—the ship in the offing. They deemed it a visit from the Manitou, coming in his big canoe, and began to prepare an entertainment for his reception. "By-and-by, the chief, *in red clothes and a glitter of metal*, with others, came ashore in a smaller canoe; mutual salutations and signs of friendship were exchanged; and after a while, strong drink was offered, which made all gay and happy. In time, as their mutual acquaintance progressed, the *white skins* told them they would stay with them, if they allowed them as much land for cultivation as the hide of a bullock, spread before them, could cover or *encompass*. The request was gratified; and the pale men, thereupon, beginning at a starting point on the hide, cut it up into one long extended narrow strip, or thong, sufficient to encompass a large place. Their cunning equally surprised and amused the confiding and simple Indians, who willingly allowed the success of their artifice, and backed it with a cordial welcome." Such was the origin of the site of New York, on the place called *Manhattan* (i. e. Manahachtanienks), a revelling name, importing "the place where they all got drunk!" and a name *then bestowed* by the Indians, as commemorative of that first great meeting.

Hudson afterwards proceeded to explore the North River, since called after his name—the *Hudson*. The Half-Moon anchored at Yonkers, and the Indians came off in canoes to traffic with the strangers. But the river narrowed beyond the Highlands, and Hudson, after sailing up as far as the site of Albany, retraced his way to Manhattan, and at once sailed for Europe. His favorable reports gave rise to an expedition of two ships in 1614, under Captains Adrian Block and Hendrick Christiaanse. It was under their auspices that the first actual settlement was begun upon the site of the present New York, consisting in the first year of *four houses*, and in the next year of a redoubt on the site of the Bowling Green. To this small village they gave the name of New Amsterdam. The settlement was of a commercial and military character, having for its object the traffic in the *fur trade*.

At the time *Holland* projected this scheme of commercial settlement, she possessed 20,000 vessels and 100,000 mariners. The city of Amsterdam was at the head of the enterprise.

From its earliest period, "Nieuw Amsterdam" had a checkered history. The English turned towards it a wistful eye, and took it from the Dutch in 1664, who succeeded, however, in recovering it in 1673. Not more than a year after, it was ceded again to the British, and underwent a change of name, from New Amsterdam to New York, in honor of James, duke of York, to whom it was made over by Charles the Second. From this period it began to make progress, although slowly, in buildings, population, and municipal arrangements.

The city, prior to British rule (that is in 1656), was laid out in streets, some of them crooked enough, and contained "one hundred and twenty houses with extensive garden lots," and about one thousand inhabitants. In 1677, another estimate reports that it comprised three hundred and sixty-eight houses, while its assessed property amounted to ninety-five thousand pounds sterling.

During the military rule of Governor Colve, who held the city for one year under the above-mentioned capture, for the States of Holland, every thing partook of a military character, and the laws still in preservation at Albany show the energy of a rigorous discipline. Then the Dutch mayor, at the head of the city militia, held his daily parades before the City Hall (Stadt Huys), then at Coenties Slip; and every evening at sunset, he received from the principal guard of the fort, called the *hoofd-wagt*, the keys of the city, and thereupon proceeded with a guard of six, to lock the city gates; then to place a *burger-wagt*—a citizen guard, as night-watch, at assigned places. The same mayors also went the rounds at sunrise to open the gates, and to restore the keys to the officers of the fort.

In 1683, the first constitutional assembly, consisting of a council of ten, and eighteen representatives, was elected, to aid in the administration of public affairs. In this year the ten original counties were organized. In 1685, on the demise of Charles II., the Duke of York ascended the throne, with the title of James II. This bigoted monarch signalized himself by forbidding the establishment of a printing-press in the colony.

Gov. Dongan was far better than his sovereign, and at length was recalled in consequence of his remonstrances against other arbitrary measures he was instructed to carry out with regard to the confederate

Indian tribes and the Jesuits. Andros was appointed to supersede him, but his also was but a short reign, for the populace grew disaffected, and in a civil commotion, one Jacob Leisler, a Dutch merchant, was proclaimed leader, and ultimately invested with the reins of government.

He also summoned a convention of deputies, from those portions of the province over which his influence extended. This convention levied taxes, and adopted other measures, for the temporary government of the colony; and thus for the first time in its existence, was the colony of New York under a free government. The strong prejudices, however, which had been awakened by Leisler's measures, soon produced in the minds of his adversaries a rancorous bitterness, which was, perhaps, never surpassed in the annals of any political controversy.

This condition of things existed for nearly two years. To the horrors of civil commotion, were added the miseries of hostile invasion by the French in Canada.

The earliest dawn of intellectual light—for the diffusion of popular intelligence had been heretofore wholly neglected—was the establishment of a free Grammar School in 1702. In 1725, the first newspaper made its appearance; and four years later, the city received the donation of a Public Library of 1642 volumes, from England. In 1732, a public Classical Academy was founded by law; and with the advance of general intelligence came a higher appreciation of popular rights. But New York was destined to be convulsed by a series of commotions; and among them the memorable one known as the Negro Plot, which resulted in a great destruction of life.

The trade of New York increased. Her ships were already seen in many foreign ports; neither Boston nor Philadelphia surpassed her in the extent of her commercial operations. Provisions, linseed-oil, furs, lumber, and iron, were the principal exports. From 1749 to 1750, two hundred and eighty-six vessels left

New York, with cargoes principally of flour and grain. In 1755, nearly thirteen thousand hogsheads of flax seed were shipped abroad.

The relations of the colonies with the mother country were assuming a serious aspect. In 1765, a congress of delegates met at New York, and prepared a declaration of their rights and grievances. The arrival of the stamped paper, so notorious in the colonial annals of America, towards the end of this year, marked the commencement of a series of explosions that were not to terminate until the city and colony of New York, in common with the other colonies, were forever rent from the dominion of Great Britain. The non-importation agreements of the merchants of New York, and other places, in 1768, were followed by stringent measures on the part of the British government. War was the result.

On the 28th of June, 1776, the British army and fleet, which had been driven from the city and harbor of Boston, entered the southern bay of New York. The troops were landed upon Staten Island. On the 22d of August, the British forces crossed the Narrows and encamped near Brooklyn, where the American army was stationed. The battle of Long Island ensued, in which, owing to unfortunate circumstances, the Americans were entirely defeated. Washington, with consummate skill, crossed the river the succeeding night, without observation; but the previous disasters, and the subsequent successful landing of the British troops at Kip's Bay, rendered it impossible to save the city.

For eight years New York was the head-quarters of the British troops, and the prison-house of American captives. Public buildings were despoiled, and churches converted into hospitals and prisons. A fire in 1776, sweeping along both sides of Broadway, destroyed one eighth of the buildings of New York.

On the 25th of November, 1783, the forces of Great Britain evacuated the city, and Washington and the

Governor of the State made a public and triumphal entry.

This important national event, forming the brightest day in the American calendar, is annually celebrated with appropriate military pomp and parade.

In ten years after the war of independence, New York had doubled its inhabitants. Yet the city had repeatedly suffered from the scourge of the yellow fever, from calamitous fires, &c. Notwithstanding all, its commercial enterprise has been rapidly and largely increasing, while its shipping has gallantly spread over every sea, and won the admiration of the world. The first establishment of regular lines of packets to Europe originated with New York, and it is also claimed for her the honor of the first experiments in steam-navigation.

Improvements hitherto had been principally connected with foreign commerce. But an impulse was now to be given to inland trade by the adoption of an extensive system of canal-navigation. Several smaller works were cast into the shade by the completion of the gigantic Erie Canal, in 1825. The union of the Atlantic with the Lakes, was announced by the firing of cannon along the whole line of the canal and of the Hudson, and was celebrated at New York by a magnificent aquatic procession, which, to indicate more clearly the navigable communication that had been opened, deposited in the ocean a portion of the waters of Lake Erie.

Municipal history is a narrative of alternate successes and reverses. For many years nothing had occurred to mar the prosperity of the city. Again misfortune came. In 1832 the Asiatic cholera appeared, and 4360 fell victims to the disease. This calamity had scarcely passed, when the great fire of 1835 destroyed, in one night, more than 600 buildings, and property to the value of over $20,000,000. The city had not recovered from the effects of this disaster, when the commercial revulsions of 1836 and 1837 shook public and private credit to their centre, and involved many of the most wealthy houses of New York in hopeless bankruptcy.

The completion of the Croton Aqueduct, in 1842, removed the inconvenience of a deficiency of water, and left an imperishable monument to the glory of New York.

A temporary check in the progress of the city was sustained by the great fire of 1845, which destroyed property to the extent of about $7,000,000; but shortly afterwards a new and vigorous impulse was again given to the commercial enterprise of the metropolis, by the constant influx of gold from the seeming exhaustless resources of the *El Dorado* of the Pacific.

GENERAL VIEW.

The City of New York, from its geographical position, having become tne great centre of commercial enterprise, is justly regarded as the Metropolitan City of the New World. In mercantile importance it bears the same relation to the United States that London does to Great Britain. Its past history is replete with interest, for it has been the theatre of some of the most important events that pertain to our country's memorable career: and although it possesses fewer historic shrines than are to be found in many cities of the Old World, yet its chronicles still live as treasured relics in the hearts of its people, and on the page of its national records. If we take a retrospective glance, we shall find that a little more than two centuries ago, this island of *Mannahata*—its earliest recorded name, had its birth-day of civilization in a few rude huts, and a fort situated where the Bowling Green now stands; and, in this comparatively brief interval in the lifetime of a nation, it has bounded from the infant *Dorp* or village into a noble city of palaces with its half million of inhabitants. It is now the great workshop of the Western world—the busy hive of industry, with its tens of thousands of artisans, mechanics, and merchants, sending out to all sections of its wide-spread domain, the magic results of machinery for all departments of handicraft, and argosies of magnificent vessels for garnering in the wealth of foreign climes.

If we glance prospectively, how shall we venture to limit its progressive march in opulence and greatness? In less than half a century hence, it will doubtless double its present numerical importance. As illustrations of the enormous increase in the value of real estate, it may be mentioned that a lot on the northwest corner of Chambers street and Broadway, was purchased by a gentleman who died in 1858, for $1000. Its present value is now estimated at no less a sum than $125,000.

The lots lately sold at auction, by Ludlow & Co., under the direction of the executors of Judge Jay, were a part of the fifteen acres bought by the late John Jay, at $500 per acre. One lot out of said purchase, situated on Broadway, we are informed has been sold within the past month for $80,000. Fabulous as is the advance from $500 per acre to $80,000 per lot, it is fully justified, as the present owner—who is now erecting a store on the lot—has refused a rent of $16,000 per year for the same.

A little more than two centuries since, the entire site of this noble city was purchased of the Indians for what was equivalent to the nominal sum of twenty-four dollars. Now the total amount of its assessed property tax is ten and a half millions of dollars. If such vast accessions of wealth have characterized the history of the past, who shall compute the constantly augmenting resources of its onward course? Half a century ago, the uses of the mighty agents of steam and the electric current were unknown: now the whole surface of our vast country is threaded over with a net-work of railroads, and our seas, lakes, and rivers are thickly studded with steamers; stately vessels, freighted with the fruits of commerce, all tending to this city as the central mart of trade. Half a century ago it took weeks to transmit news from New York to New Orleans—now our communications are conveyed over the length and breadth of the land almost with the velocity of the lightning's flash. Within a like interval the most rapid printing-press was slowly worked by hand-power—now the winged messengers of intelligence are multiplied with the marvellous rapidity of 60,000 copies an hour. While the mechanic arts have thus revolutionized the social condition of the past, a corresponding change has marked its history, in the establishment of numerous schools of learning—diffusing their beneficent influence on the minds and morals of the masses.

Then, again, as respects its costly stores and private residences, New York seems to vie with London and Paris. All along Broadway, and its intersecting streets, the eye is greeted everywhere by long lines of marble and stone buildings, many of them of great architectural elegance. The several broad Avenues and Squares, in the upper part of the city, are studded with a succession of splendid mansions—in some instances costing from $50,000 to $200,000 each. There are, it is estimated, some three hundred churches, many of them of costly and magnificent proportions; while its superb hotels—the boast of the metropolis—are, in some instances, capable of accommodating about one thousand guests.

How mighty and far-reaching must its influence become in its future progress, it were difficult to compute: since its numerical extent, numbering at present, if we include Brooklyn and the adjacent places on the west, over a million of souls, will ere long place it, in the scale of cities of the world, in the foremost rank.

BROADWAY, LOOKING UP FROM EXCHANGE PLACE.

NEW YORK AS IT IS.

Society in New York has many phases—it is cosmopolitan—an amalgam, composed of all imaginable varieties and shades of character. It is a confluence of many streams, whose waters are ever turbid and confused in their rushing to this great vortex. What incongruous elements are here commingled,—the rude and the refined, the sordid and the self-sacrificing, the religious and the profane, the learned and the illiterate, the affluent and the destitute, the thinker and the doer, the virtuous and the ignoble, the young and the aged—all nations, dialects, and sympathies—all habits, manners, and customs of the civilized globe.

City life everywhere presents protean aspects; let us take a glance at some of its more striking features, notwithstanding the mixed multitudes that are incessantly thronging its various avenues. There are yet certain localities that exhibit distinct characteristics: life in Wall-street presents an epitomized view of its mercantile phase. Here are its banks, its money-exchangers, and their great place of rendezvous, the Exchange; beneath the dome of which many mighty projects have had their birth. Here have been concocted vast schemes of commercial enterprise, and here, too, have originated many noble acts of public benefaction.

Up Nassau street, to its junction with Chatham street, of mock-auction notoriety, we catch a glimpse of another phase of city life. To denizens of New

York, society is usually known under the generic divisions of *Broadway* and *Bowery*. Each has its distinct idiosyncracies: the former being regarded as patrician, and the latter as plebeian. Looking at New York longitudinally, we may say that Canal street, at present, marks the boundary of the great workshop. In the precincts of Union Square and Madison Square, and especially the Fifth Avenue, we find the monuments of the wealth, taste, and splendor of its citizens.

The southern part of the city—its original site—exhibits all kinds of irregularity—the streets are narrow, sinuous and uneven in their surface; but the northern or upper portion is laid out in right angles. There are some twelve fine avenues, at parallel distances apart of about 800 feet. There are about 200 miles of paved streets in the Metropolis, extending to Forty-fourth street; exclusive of projected streets not yet paved, over 100 streets more. The city has been laid out and surveyed to the extent of 12 miles from the Battery. The portion occupied exceeds in circumference more than extent.

Perhaps the densest parts of the Metropolis,—its very heart, from whence issues the vitalizing tide of its commerce,—is the junction of Nassau and Fulton streets, and its vicinity. The collision of interests which all the stir and traffic of these crowded scenes involve, brings human nature into strong relief, and intensifies the lights and shades of character.

It is in these dusty avenues to wealth—these vestibules where fraud contends with honor for an entrance into the temple, that we read the heart of man better than in books.

The great characteristic of New York is din and excitement,—every thing is done in a hurry—all is intense anxiety. It is especially noticeable in the leading thoroughfare of Broadway; where the noise and confusion caused by the incessant passing and repassing of some 18,000 vehicles a day, render it a Babel scene of confusion.

New York has been ever and justly renowned for its catholic and liberal public benefactions and charities. Among her many glories, this is most conspicuous. New York may be called the asylum for the oppressed and distressed of all nations. Abounding in beneficent institutions suited to the relief of the various "ills that flesh is heir to," and enriched with the most liberal endowments for classical and popular instruction, she bears the palm in all that pertains to the moral, intellectual, and physical advancement of society. It is true we are a mercantile and money-making people, but the empire city is an illustration of some of its noblest uses.

By way of introduction to the city in detail, we recommend the visitor first to get a bird's-eye view of it from the steeple of Trinity church. A view from this elevation, over 320 feet in height, affords a good idea of the general extent and topography of the city. The tower is accessible to the public at any time of the day, excepting the hours devoted to divine service, morning and afternoon. To facilitate the ascent of the church tower there are landing-places; at the first of these you have a fine view of the interior of this Cathedral-like edifice. At the next resting-place is the belfry, with its solemn chimes: here too is a balcony allowing us a first view of the city. Still higher up we gain a magnificent panoramic view of all we have left below us,—which amply repays our toilsome tour of many steps. The variegated scene stretches out in every direction, with new beauties,—north and south lies Broadway with its teeming multitudes and its numberless vehicles; west and east are crowded streets of house-tops terminating only with the waters of the inclosing rivers. Looking eastward, we see Wall street immediately below us, with the Treasury Building on the left, and a little further on the right the Custom-house, the Wall-street ferry, and the East River which separates New York from Brooklyn; with the New York bay stretching to the southeast.

Sandy Hook, the Highlands of Neversink, and the coast of Staten Island. To the northeast, the eastern district of Brooklyn, formerly known as Williamsburg, the Navy Yard, &c., and still further to the north, the rocky channel called Hurl-gate,—so perilous to our Dutch forefathers; near by Randall and Blackwell's Islands, with their City Asylums. Transferring our gaze to Broadway, we notice on the corner of Wall street the Bank of the Republic, and on the next street the Metropolitan Bank. Passing several fine marble buildings, we notice Barnum's Museum on the east side of Broadway, and opposite to it St. Paul's Church, then the Astor House, the Park, and the City Hall; the brown-stone building on the east side being that of the Times Office. Beyond the City Hall inclosure is Stewart's marble palace, then the City Hospital, surrounded with trees, and opposite it, Judge Whiting's fine marble building; further north are numerous elegant stores, including Brooks' brownstone structure, Lord & Taylor's marble edifice, St. Nicholas Hotel, the Metropolitan, and still further on in the distance, Grace Church, with its beautiful white spire, Union Park, &c.

Turning to the opposite point of view, the Hudson river, with Jersey City, and Hoboken, with its beautiful walks, its distant hills and valleys; on this side of the river, the steamers, ships, and docks. This superb river has been often compared with the Rhine for its picturesque beauty, we can here get but a faint idea of it, for its bold scenery is seen only after journeying some 40 miles to the north, we catch merely a glimpse of the Palisades, beginning at Weehawken and extending about 20 miles. Veering to the south, we see the fortified islets of the lower bay, with Staten Island, Richmond, &c., with their numerous picturesque cottages, villas, and castellated mansions, and to the southwest, the Raritan bay, the Passaic river, leading to Newark in the distance, &c.

PARKS AND PUBLIC SQUARES.

BATTERY.

Commencing our descriptions of the notabilia of New-York with its pleasure-grounds and parks, we ought first to mention the *Battery*, situated at the southernmost terminus of the metropolis. These grounds cover an area of about twelve acres, of the crescent form, having a profusion of stately trees, which afford a delightful place of retreat in the summer-time, for pleasure-seekers, who prefer to inhale the fresh sea-breeze under their shade to the crowded throngs of fashion in the city. The walks stretching along the margin of these grounds were formerly much frequented, but of late years, in consequence of the rapid growth of the city, all private residences having been transferred to the upper or northern part of the city, are consequently now not so much an object of attraction. Connected with the Battery is Castle Garden. Originally a fortification, it was subsequently let on lease as a place of public amusement. It was probably the largest audience-room in the world. It was the scene of Jenny Lind's first appearance in America. This building has now little architectural beauty to boast; having been for some time used as a depot for emigrants. The grounds of the Battery have been needlessly extended within the last few years at an enormous expense to the city.

BOWLING GREEN.

Close to the Battery, at the entrance to Broadway, is the small inclosure so called, from having been used as such prior to the Revolution. At that time it contained a leaden equestrian statue of George III., which the populace in their patriotic zeal demolished, and converted into musket-balls. On this site there is now a fountain, which is during summer to be seen bubbling up with the clear waters of the Croton.

THE PARK

Is a triangular inclosure of about 11 acres, containing the City Hall and other public buildings. At the southern part there is a beautiful fountain, inclosed in a basin 100 feet in diameter. The iron is in the shape of an Egyptian lily, around it are numerous perforations through which small jets of water are projected, which descending form a mist, while the main jet throws up a column of water to a great height, amidst the surrounding trees.

ST. JOHN'S PARK,

Or HUDSON SQUARE, situated between Laight, Varick, and Hudson streets, is a small, but beautiful inclosure thickly planted with lofty trees. It is the property of the vestry of Trinity Church.

WASHINGTON SQUARE,

Formerly the site of a Potter's Field, occupies about nine acres, and is decorated with numerous gravel-walks, and an elegant fountain in the centre of the grounds. It forms a pleasant up-town park, situated a little to the west of Broadway, between Fourth and Eighth streets. It is surrounded by rows of fine buildings—private residences on each side, and at the east end by the New York University and Dr. Hutton's Church—each fine Gothic structures.

UNION PARK

Is in Union Square, at the upper or northern en of Broadway—extending from 14th to 17th streets. This pleasure-ground is inclosed by a handsome iron railing, and contains a variety of fine trees, gravel-

CITY HALL.

walks, and also a fountain. At the south side is the bronze equestrian statue of Washington and the Union Place Hotel, at the opposite extremity are the Everett House and the Clarendon, and at the western side, Dr. Cheever's Church and the Spingler Hotel.

GRAMERCY PARK,

Situated a little to the northeast of the above, is a select and beautiful inclosure on a smaller scale. This park is private property, having been ceded to the owners of the surrounding lots by S. B. Ruggles, Esq. It forms the area between 20th and 21st streets, and the 3d and 4th Avenues.

STUYVESANT PARK

Extends from 15th to 17th streets, and is divided by the intersecting passage of the Second Avenue. The Rev. Dr. Tyng's Church is upon the west side of this park. The ground was presented by the late P. G. Stuyvesant, Esq., to the corporation of the church.

TOMPKINS SQUARE

Is one of the largest parks of the city. It occupies the area formed by Avenues A and B, and 7th and 10th streets.

MADISON SQUARE,

Comprising 10 acres, is at the junction of Broadway and Fifth Avenue. On the west side stands the monument of General Worth. The houses surrounding this park include some of the most elegant of the city.

CENTRAL PARK.

This great pleasure-ground of the city may be reached by most of the city railroads, and as each entrance has its own peculiar attractions, strangers will naturally take the cars that are most convenient for them. At the gates on 59th Street, at 6th, 7th, and 8th Avenues, and at 72d Street, on the 5th Avenue, carriages are generally standing for hire: not being under the control of the Park Commissioners, they are not responsible for their regulation and management.

If you close with the offer of one of the owners of these carriages to "take you all around the Park," you must not conclude that you have seen the attractions. Should the driver take you over all the drives, you have not seen the full attractions of the Park; they can be seen only by taking the foot-paths, and the visitor should, if possible, take more than one day for it. The extent of the walks and the number of things to be seen are sufficient to afford a new and interesting walk through the Park each day for a fortnight.

The Time to go to the Park

depends upon the season of the year and upon the objects and tastes of the visitor.

The gates are open at the following hours: during the months of December, January, and February, from 7 A. M. to 8 P. M.; during March, April, May, June, October, and November, from 6 A. M. to 9 P. M.; during July, August, and September, from 5 A. M. to 11 P. M.

Those who go to see the foliage and the flowers, or on a botanical expedition, will be best satisfied from the 1st of April to the middle of November, at any time in the day. In the hottest days of the months of July, August, and September, until the trees are more fully grown, the visitor will perhaps prefer to be at the Park before 10 A. M., or after 3 P. M., but at any hour agreeable seats and shade may be found. Those who desire to see the equipages, fine turn-outs, and the gayeties of the city will go to the Park from April to November, from 3 P. M. to 7 P. M. In the warm months the fashion is at the Park from 5 to 7.30 P. M. In the season, June to October, the well-selected and thoroughly accomplished band of the Park plays at the music pavilion on the mall, on Saturday afternoons, free to all. The pieces performed include popular national airs, and the best new music that appears in Europe or America. Every pains is taken to maintain a high standard of these musical entertainments.

In the skating season, December to March, the greatest numbers are at the Park after 3 P. M., but many persons are on the ice in the morning and through the day. When the ice is in good condition a ball is hoisted on the arsenal building, and generally the city cars indicate by small flags when the skating is good.

The Park is a parallelogram, bounded on the South by 59th Street, on the North by 110th Street, on the East by the 5th Avenue, and the West by the 8th Avenue, containing, including the reservoirs, 843 acres. It is about 2½ miles long, and half a mile in width; it is intersected by four transverse roads, which are laid at a lower level to accommodate the business traffic of the city; without interfering with the pleasure travel. The Park was originally a bare, unwholesome suburb of the city, acres of it were naked of soil, and stagnant, marshy spots gathered the filth of bone-boiling establishments and pig-styes. The change to its present beauty has been accomplished in an almost inconceivable short period of time. Work was commenced on the place in 1858, and in one year thereafter a part was thrown open to public use, to which other completed portions have since been added, from time to time, as completed.

The Central Park is larger than any park on this continent, larger than any of the London parks, and with three exceptions larger than any city park in the world. These exceptions are the Bois de Boulogne at Paris, the Prater at Vienna, and the Phenix Park at Dublin.

There are in it about 9 miles of carriage drive, 4 of bridle road, and about 25 miles of walk. Intersections of lines of travel are made by archways, to avoid danger. Every effort has been made to preserve the natural features of the Park.

More than 260,000 trees and shrubs of all kinds have already been planted, and the work is still going on. The grounds are laid out on a plan: the system of walks will conduct the visitor from one end of the Park to the other, and bring him in view of most of the objects desirable to be seen.

It possesses already the several essentials of a picturesque park—pond, stream, hill, rock, plain, and slope. The ridge which rises near the Battery, and forms the back-bone of the Island of Manhattan, traverses the Park from end to end; forming, in its course, at least two admirable points of view, from which delicious views of the adjacent scenery may be obtained. Through the valleys beneath course little brooks, which, with the help of thorough drainage, have been swelled into considerable streams, while a swamp has been converted by skilful engineering into a lake of one hundred acres, serving as one of the receiving reservoirs of the city. There are hills, too, with rough, rocky sides, which will pass, with a little trimming, for mountain scenery; and there are passes, which, with appropriate foliage, may almost figure as Alpine valleys. From botanical surveys already made, it appears that the ground is adapted to the cultivation of an unusual variety of plants and flowers. In fact, so many and so various are the charms of this beautiful resort, that, although it is visited annually by hundreds of thousands of persons, it may still be said that it is not yet fully and justly appreciated by those who live within reach of its enjoyments; and one object which we have in view in giving a fuller synopsis of its attractions, is to induce the tired resident of the city to avail himself more frequently of this retreat. As a place of education, a pleasant school for the instruction of the taste, the value of the Park can scarcely be exaggerated.

The Terrace is the principal architectural structure. This terminates the Mall on the north; below it is the explanade surrounding the main fountain. The visitor will be well repaid by the examination of the design and execution of the detail of the stone work of the terrace: to the Mall all of the walks of the lower park lead; the walks at all the entrance gates on 59th street will lead to it under the marble arch. But we must answer the question:

How are we to get there?

The cars of the Second, Third, Sixth, and Eighth Avenue railroads, stopping either at 65th street, which leads to that portion of the Park known as the "Green," or at 79th street, leading to the "Ramble," afford convenient access; to which means of conveyance may be added the various stage lines which carry passengers to within a few blocks of the Park. The cars should always be avoided by those who are unwilling to pay for the privilege of standing up.

Whither to go after reaching the Park.

The principal walks of the lower park lead more or less directly to the Mall Terrace, and through this to the Terrace, which is the central architectural feature of the plan. The attractions of this spot are perhaps as great as any within the limits of the Park, and from it we may take a view of the scene before us, and may note especially

The Archways and Bridges,

which are objects of admiration to the visitor, and are about thirty in number, of great beauty and variety of form and material, no two of the entire number being alike. Passing from the Terrace to the Fountain and Bow Bridge, we find ourselves among the attractions of the

Ramble,

of which a good view can be had from the hill which rises about forty yards distant from the Bow Bridge, and commands a fair prospect of the lower park. But the beauties of this place must be explored by the tasteful visitor, who will admire, in turn, the paths leading along the shore, the bold projections of rock, the well-arranged contrivances for rural effect, and, above all, the intermingled beauties of wood and water, verdure and rock. A charming view of the entire area of the Park may be had from the

Hill

that rises on the south side of the old reservoir, and attains an eminence surpassing that of any other point. From this we have the whole lower park lying in full view for a mile below us: the Lake and the Ramble are almost at our feet; the Croton Reservoirs are close to us on the north; and a mile and a quarter away is seen a pile of brick and painted wood, now used as a hospital for U. S. soldiers—being more than a quarter of a mile this side of its northern boundary. Still further beyond, we see the High Bridge—Westchester County—and the East River.

Under the rock on which we are standing passes one of the

Sub-ways,

or *transverse-roads*, as they are less descriptively called in the nomenclature of the Park. These are of infinite importance to the beauty and convenience of the arrangements, as they allow the travel incident to business to pass unhindered on its way, crossing the park at four places, viz., at 65th, 79th, 85th, 97th streets; while no impediment is suffered by the pleasure-seekers, who are left in the uninterrupted enjoyment of their rides, drives, or walks. Much credit has been given, both in this country and in Europe, to the architects of the Park for the clever suggestion of these useful roads.

The Upper Park

is the most bold and romantic, and at the same time the richest in its historical associations. It is said that "the deep valley called McGowan's Pass, dividing this northern portion, is the valley which by means of its darkly wooded hillsides sheltered the secret messengers passing between the scattered parties of the American troops who, during the few days intervening between their disheartening rout on Long Island and the battle of Harlem Plains, rallied about the range of hills extending from Fort Washington to Bloomingdale." A portion of the "Old Boston Road," venerable as being the oldest road out of New York, on the east side of the island, is still visible in the northeastern section of the Park. It should, if possible, be suffered to remain as an interesting and precious relic of the past. It was by this road that the Huguenot refugees, living in New Rochelle, came into the city to attend the services at the French Church on Sunday.

Miscellaneous Items.—The soil is composed for the most part of diluvial deposits, in which are many boulders (mainly trap rock), and the debris of the gneiss rock.

The lowest point, about 109th street and Fifth Avenue, is less than 2 feet above the tide; the highest, at 83d street, near Eighth Avenue, is 138 feet above the tide.

Urinals are located at convenient points about the grounds.

Cottages for ladies are also located about the grounds. each in charge of a female attendant, whose duty it is to wait upon visitors, to aid them in case of illness, and to keep every thing in order in the place of which she has charge.

To avoid accidents, persons on foot should keep on the walks, and not walk in the ride or drive.

Visitors are requested

Not to walk on the *grass*, except in those places where the word *common* is posted,

Not to pick any Flower, Leaf, Twig, or Fruit,

Not to deface or mark the seats or other structures,

Not to throw stones or other missiles,

Not to annoy the Birds,

Not to offer any thing for sale.

At each gate stands a gate-keeper, and on the grounds will be found Park Keepers, in uniform, who are required to give information about the Park to visitors, and to deport themselves with politeness to all.

No person employed at the Park is allowed to receive any pay or reward for his services. They are amply paid for the performance of their duties. For lost articles apply to the Property Clerk, in the old arsenal building.

The Park is under the management of a Board of Commissioners, composed of the following gentlemen: Henry G. Stebbins, President; R. M. Blatchford; Charles H. Russell; Waldo Hutchins; Thos. C. Fields, Secretary; Moses H. Grinnell; John F. Butterworth; Andrew H. Green.

The chief executive officer of the Board is Andrew H. Green, the Comptroller of the Park.

The office of the Board is at No. 31 Nassau Street.

Custom House.

THE CITY HALL.

This is an imposing edifice, and, for the most part, built of marble. It was constructed between the years 1803–10. At the celebration of the Atlantic Telegraph, the clock-tower and other upper portions of the building were destroyed by fire, but have since been rebuilt.

Previous to the completion of the new cupola, our City Fathers contracted with Messrs. Sperry & Co., the celebrated tower-clock makers of Broadway, to build a clock for it, at a cost not exceeding $4,000, that our citizens might place the utmost reliance upon, as a time-keeper of unvarying correctness. During the month of April the clock was completed, and the busy thousands who were daily wont to look up to the silent monitor, above which the figure of justice was enthroned, hailed its appearance with the utmost satisfaction. It is undoubtedly the finest specimen of a tower clock on this side of the Atlantic, and as an accurate time-keeper competent judges pronounce it to be unsurpassed in the world. The main wheels are thirty inches in diameter, the escapement is jeweled, and the pendulum, which is in itself a curiosity, is over fourteen feet in length. It is a curious fact that the pendulum bob weighs over 300 pounds; but so finely finished is every wheel, pinion and pivot in the clock, and so little power is required to drive them, that a weight of only 100 pounds is all that is necessary to keep this ponderous mass of metal vibrating, and turn four pairs of hands on the dials of the cupola! The clock does not stand, as many suppose, directly behind the dials, but in the story below, and a perpendicular iron rod twenty-five feet in length connects it with the dial-works above.

In the building are the several offices of the Mayor, Common Council and Aldermen, the Governor's room, City Library, and other business offices.

The United States District Court is located in Chambers street, at the rear of the City Hall. The several other Courts are held in the brown stone building, situated at the northeast angle of the City Hall.

THE CUSTOM-HOUSE,

Occupying the building which was formerly the Merchants' Exchange, is located between Wall street, Exchange Place, William and Hanover streets. The material employed in its construction is blue Quincy granite, and it is characterized by fine proportions, and massive, substantial appearance. Its dimensions are on such a scale as to produce a fine architectural effect, being in length, 200 feet; in width, from 144 to 171; while it has an elevation of 77 feet at the cornice, and 124 feet at the top of the dome. The portico of eighteen Ionic columns, which graces its front, imparts to it an imposing effect. The interior of the building fully sustains the impression; for besides the numerous apartments set apart to various uses, it contains a rotunda in the centre, surmounted by a lofty dome, which is supported, in part, by eight Corinthian columns of Italian marble. This rotunda is capable of containing 3000 persons. Its entire cost, including the ground, was over $1,800,000. The architect was Isaiah Rogers; and it was built on the site of the old Exchange, destroyed by the fire of 1835. The original stockholders lost every penny of their investment, it having been sold to other hands to defray the mortgage held by the Barings of London.

THE MERCHANTS' EXCHANGE

Is now held in William street, near Exchange Place. The Merchants' Exchange sales-room is in the Trinity Building, on Broadway, north of Trinity Church.

THE POST-OFFICE,

In Nassau street, between Cedar and Liberty streets, was formerly the Middle Dutch Church. At a time—namely, during the war of the Revolution—when most

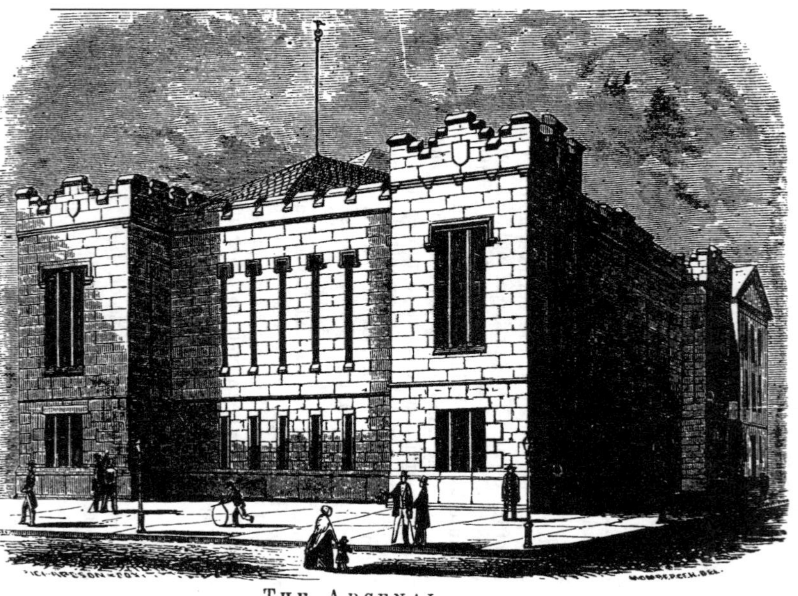

THE ARSENAL.

of the churches were turned to military use by the British, this one sustained the greatest injuries; which more or less, however, fell upon all. In 1790, it received such repairs as fitted it again for public worship; but it was afterwards secured by the government and devoted to its present use,—that of a post-office. Its internal arrangements are extensive, and well adapted to the objects of its present use; the postmaster's room is so situated as to command a view of all that is going on in the building. It was in the old wooden steeple of this building that Franklin practised his experiments in electricity.

THE UNITED STATES TREASURY AND ASSAY OFFICE,

On the corner of Wall and Nassau streets, is a splendid building, constructed in the Doric order of Grecian architecture. It is built in the most substantial manner of white marble, something after the model of the Parthenon at Athens; as a piece of masonry, it is equal to any structure extant, and to judge from appearances, likely to become as enduring as the pyramids; it occupies the site of the old Federal Hall. The building is 200 feet long, 80 feet wide, and 80 feet high: at the southern end, on Wall street, is a portico of eight purely Grecian columns, 5 feet 8 inches in diameter, and 32 feet high; and on the northern end, on Pine street, is a corresponding portico, of similar columns. The front portico is ascended by eighteen marble steps, and the rear portico, on Pine street, by only three or four marble steps. It is two lofty stories high above the basement story. The great business hall is a splendid room, 60 feet in diameter. The cost of the building, including the ground, was $1,195,000.

THE CITY ARMORY.

The old City Armory or Arsenal, is situated at the junction of Elm and White streets, extending 84 feet on

Elm, and 31 feet on White street. The edifice is so constructed, that in case of any popular tumult, it could be defended by a garrison of 50 men. The ground-floor is used as a gun-room, and the upper room for drilling, &c. The style of the architecture is a kind of gothic, with castellated towers. This arsenal contains a portion of the artillery of the first division of the New York State Militia. It is intended that a large flagstaff shall be erected on the centre of the roof of this building, in order that telegraphic communications may be conveyed by wires from it to the new arsenal up town, which is situated on the corner of Thirty-fifth street and Seventh Avenue.

THE HALL OF RECORDS,

Located to the east of the City Hall, was originally used for a prison, and subsequently as a cholera hospital. It is of coarse stone stuccoed over; the entrances north and south, are ornamented with Ionic columns. The building is now used as the Depository for Deeds, Records, &c.

THE HALLS OF JUSTICE.

This is the city prison, or as it is more familiarly styled, from its gloomy aspect, "the Tombs." It is a spacious building, or rather series of buildings,—occupying the square bounded by Centre street on the east, Elm street on the west, and Franklin and Leonard streets on the north and south. It is a massive structure, in the Egyptian style, the main entrance being by an ascent of steps beneath a large portico supported by massive Egyptian columns. The Court of Sessions, Police Court, and others, are held in this building. It also comprises the prison, which has about 150 cells. The house of detention measures 142 feet by 45. The place of execution of criminals is the interior courtyard. The edifice was completed in 1838. On application to the keeper, visitors may obtain admission to the building.

THE TOMBS.

BENEVOLENT INSTITUTIONS.

BLACKWELL'S ISLAND.

A visit to the several establishments on this island will well repay any one interested in the efforts for ameliorating human suffering. There are on the island, the Penitentiary, with its 500 to 1000 convicts, the Alms-House Hospital, the Lunatic Asylum, and the New Work-House,—which last is one of the most complete edifices in the country. It is built of stone taken from the quarries of the island. It is a very spacious building, being capable of holding about 600 persons; all its internal arrangements are very complete. The humane object of this institution is to separate vagrants from criminals, and to compel all to work who are able to do something towards their own support. The building, which is 325 feet in length, cost about $100,000. Tickets for admission to the island can be obtained of the Secretary of the Governors of the Alms-House Department, at the Rotunda, rear of the City Hall. There are various modes of conveyance thither,—by the Second or Third Avenue cars, and by steamer which leaves foot of Grand street, East River, or by the Harlem stage from 23 Chatham street to 61st street, and cross to the island at any hour.

WARD'S ISLAND

May also be visited by the same conveyances, on obtaining a permit from the Commissioners of Emigration, at their office in the New City Hall, near the junction of Chambers and Centre streets.

RANDALL'S ISLAND

May be reached also by boat from foot of Grand street each day at noon. Here are the nurseries for the support and instruction of destitute children. This institution is the most interesting of all, and commends itself to the sympathies of all who would become acquainted with the benevolent agencies of New York city. Permits may be had, as for Blackwell's Island. There are usually to be seen here, in the several instutions, from 4000 to 5000 persons young and old.

THE NEW YORK ORPHAN ASYLUM,

Situated in Bloomingdale, near Eightieth street, comprises a fine building 120 feet by 60, and nine acres ot ground, laid out with much taste. These grounds command a splendid view of the Hudson and East Rivers with the surrounding scenery. There are in this institution about 200 orphans. The institution was incorporated by charter in 1807, and its present edifice was completed in 1840. It is a most praiseworthy institution, and a very interesting one to visit.

THE BLOOMINGDALE ASYLUM FOR THE INSANE,

A branch of the New York Hospital, is situated in the Bloomingdale Road, at a distance of about seven miles from the City Hall. It occupies a most beautiful and commanding site, and its approach and surroundings are admirably fitted to lighten the sense of depression and gloom which we instinctively associate with every establishment of the kind. The treatment administered to its unfortunate inmates, too, is of the most enlightened, humane, and rational sort. The principal building is 211 feet in length, 60 in depth, and four stories in height; with side buildings.

The approach to the Asylum from the southern entrance, by the stranger who associates the most sombre scenes with a lunatic hospital, is highly pleasing. The sudden opening of the view, the extent of the grounds, the various avenues gracefully winding through so arge a lawn; the cedar hedges, the fir and other ornamental trees, tastefully distributed or grouped, the

NEW YORK HOSPITAL.

variety of shrubbery and flowers. The central building, however, is always open to visitors, and the view from the top of it, being the most extensive and beautiful of any in the vicinity of the city, is well worthy of their attention.

THE NEW YORK HOSPITAL,

Situated on Broadway, between Duane and Worth streets, is a most important benevolent institution. It dates back to 1771, when it was founded by the Earl of Dunmore, who was at that time governor of the colony. The accommodation for patients, which of late years has been greatly enlarged, is very extensive, and excellent in every respect. It is a receptacle in cases of sudden accidents. It is not altogether gratuitous; but to such as are able to pay a little, it offers most important advantages—four dollars a week commanding the best medical attendance, besides nursing and medicine. The students, too, have the benefit, for a small annual fee, of accompanying the surgeons in their rounds. The institution has an annual revenue from various sources of about $80,000, which is expended in the support of the establishment. The hospital buildings are fitted up in excellent style for the accommodation of patients.

The approach to the Hospital from Broadway is by an avenue of 90 feet wide, planted with a double row of trees. The main building is of gray stone, 124 feet long, including its two wings, by 50 feet deep. It contains separate apartments for patients afflicted with contagious diseases, possesses a theatre for surgical operations, and other apartments, and also a Marine department. The average number of patients admitted annually may be stated at 3000 to 3500. The best medical attendance is secured to this institution.

JEWS HOSPITAL

Is located at 158 West Twenty-eighth street.

4

CHILDRENS' HOSPITAL AND NURSERY,

East Fifty-first street, near Lexington Avenue.

In connection with the New York Hospital may be mentioned,

THE NEW YORK DISPENSARIES.

Which are associations for giving medicine and medical advice to the poor. The Northern Dispensary, situated on the corner of Christopher and Sixth streets, was founded in 1829; and the Eastern Dispensary, on the corner of Ludlow street and Essex Market Place, was instituted in 1834. There is also a still older Dispensary on the corner of White and Centre streets, established in 1795; and is estimated to have given relief to more than fifty thousand patients since its first organization.

THE DEMILT DISPENSARY

Is a fine building at the corner of the Second Avenue and Twenty-third street, which with the ground cost $30,000—the noble donation of the late Miss Demilt. About 3000 patients are annually benefited by this noble charity of a single benefactor.

THE ASYLUM FOR AGED INDIGENT FEMALES

Is located in Twentieth street, near Second Avenue. Its title indicates sufficiently the object of the institution, which is both well filled and well sustained.

ST. LUKE'S HOSPITAL,

At the corner of Fifth Avenue and Fiftieth street, is an admirable charity sustained by members of the Episcopal Churches of New York.

LEAKE AND WATTS ORPHAN ASYLUM,

Located between the Fourth and Fifth Avenues, and near One hundred and seventeenth street, is another worthy institution, founded by the two benevolent personages whose names it bears. The Asylum measures 206 feet front, and it has 26 acres of ground. It supports over 200 children.

• THE MAGDALEN FEMALE ASYLUM,

Situate west of the Harlem railroad, between the streets known as Eighty-eighth and Eighty-ninth streets. This praiseworthy institution, as its name indicates, has been established for the recovery and restoration of fallen and distressed females. It is well sustained; and by the self-sacrificing labors of the benevolent, has been productive of great good.

THE UNIVERSITY MEDICAL SCHOOL,

In Fourteenth street, between Irving Place and Third Avenue, has large apartments, and a regular faculty; also a library of 5000 volumes. The museum is extensive and valuable.

COLLEGE OF PHYSICIANS AND SURGEONS.

This is a handsome edifice, corner of Twenty-third street and Fourth Avenue. It was founded in 1807, has eight professors and about two hundred students. There is a small library here, of about 1500 volumes, and an anatomical museum. These museums are accessible to the public on application to the janitor.

NEW YORK MEDICAL COLLEGE

Is located at No. 90 East Thirteenth street; it was chartered in 1850, and is devoted to the instruction of young medical practitioners. It possesses a valuable anatomical museum, chemical laboratory, &c. There is also in this building the *College of Pharmacy.*

THE INSTITUTION FOR THE DEAF AND DUMB.

This noble and well-conducted Asylum is situated at Fanwood, Washington Heights, near 150th street, which is reached by means of the Hudson River railroad. The principal building measures 110 feet by 60, and is five stories high. It is capable of accommodating from 200 to 300 pupils, exclusive of the principal and teachers, &c. It is one of the best-endowed institutions of benevolence in New York; being sustained by appropriations made by the State Legislature, by the City Corporation, and private benefactions. The pupils are instructed in the ordinary branches of learning, and some of them in the various trades. Dr. Peet is the superintendent. Open to the public from half-past one to four P. M. every day.

THE INSTITUTION FOR THE BLIND

Is on the Ninth Avenue, between Thirty-third and Thirty-fourth streets, occupying 32 lots of ground, presented by James Boorman, Esq. The edifice is of granite, and of the Gothic order of architecture. It owes its origin mainly to Dr. J. D. Russ, whose attention was directed to the sightless condition of a large number of the children in the City Alms House. Moved by the spectacle, he determined to devote himself to their relief, and for that purpose took seven children from the Alms House and gratuitously instructed them for nearly two years, and finally obtained the passage of an act by the legislature for their support. In this effort he was ably supported by Samuel Wood, a well-known member of the Society of Friends, and Dr. Samuel Akerly, distinguished for his zeal and labors in behalf of the Institution for the Deaf and Dumb. Here also the usual branches of education are taught, and the pupils are instructed in the several useful arts of life. It is an exceedingly useful object to visit, as is also the Deaf and Dumb Asylum. The Institution is open to visitors on week days, from one to six P. M., and may be conveniently reached by stages and cars that run on the Eighth Avenue.

THE HOUSE OF INDUSTRY AND HOME FOR THE FRIENDLESS

Is located on Thirtieth street, between Fourth and Madison Avenues. It is under the direction of a society devoted to the protection of deserted children, and adult persons who may be in distress. This association has largely contributed to the relief of the poor and destitute of the city,—in one year it relieved, and provided with places, over 600 young and old. The society publishes a paper semi-monthly, entitled "*The Advocate and Guardian*," which has a circulation of about 15,000 copies; it has also published over 10,000 tracts, &c.

THE HOUSE AND SCHOOL OF INDUSTRY

Has its rooms No. 100 West Sixteenth street. It was organized in 1850.

THE SOCIETY FOR THE RELIEF OF POOR WIDOWS WITH SMALL CHILDREN,

Was organized in 1797, by the efforts of the late Mrs. Isabella Graham. Its average number of persons relieved, is about 200 widows and 500 children. Mrs. L. Perkins, 1st Directress, 78 West Fourteenth street.

THE HOUSE OF INDUSTRY,

In the Five Points, near Centre and Pearl streets, conducted by the Rev. Mr. Pease, is another praiseworthy institution. Placed in the very midst of squalid poverty and crime, this excellent charity has achieved great results in rescuing and reclaiming the youth of vicious parentage. Mr. Pease's institution dates back only to 1848, yet thus far has its progress been incomparably the most successful of any of the numerous noble charities of New York. Persevering through numberless difficulties, Mr. Pease at length has achieved a great success in his laudable endeavors. He has now from 100 to 200 inmates, rescued from the purlieus of vice

4*

and poverty; hopefully engaged in his "House of Industry." Since its foundation, between 800 and 900 women have been sent out to places in the country. By his economical plan, the major part of the expenses of the establishment have been defrayed by the productive labor of the inmates.

There are many other philanthropic societies in New York, which it is not necessary to detail, as they may be found briefly named in the City Directory. The more prominent are the following benevolent societies:

ODD FELLOWS HALL.

The Independent Order of Odd Fellows number, in New York city, about 90 lodges, and about 12 encampments, including many thousand members; many of the lodges have fine halls, in various parts of this city and the neighboring cities of Brooklyn, Williamsburg, Jersey City, &c.; but the grand rendezvous of the order, is the large brown-stone building at the corner of Grand and Centre streets, erected at a cost of $125,000. This imposing edifice presents a noble appearance, being substantially built, lofty, and surmounted by a dome. It contains a series of highly ornamented lodge-rooms, richly furnished and in different styles of architecture: some Egyptian, Grecian, Elizabethan, &c. These elegant apartments are well worth a visit. The average receipts of the association which owns this edifice, is estimated at about $75,000. Their distribution in the form of benefactions to the sick and poor, is on a scale of corresponding liberality.

ANCIENT AND HONORABLE FRATERNITY OF FREE AND ACCEPTED MASONS.

The M. W. Grand Lodge of the ancient and honorable fraternity of Free and Accepted Masons of the State of New York, meets at such commodious place as may be appointed on the 1st Tuesday in March, June, September, and December. Subordinate lodges meet every evening in Crosby street, corner of Broome street, and at Odd Fellows Hall, Grand and Centre streets.

THE SAILORS SNUG HARBOR,

An Asylum for aged and infirm seamen, is situated on the north side of Staten Island. It was founded by Capt. Randall in 1801, and incorporated in 1806 in New York; the present noble building on Staten Island, measures 225 feet in length, with 160 acres of ground; about 300 aged and disabled seamen are here supported. Near the Quarantine grounds, are the *Seamen's Retreat* for the sick, and the *Home for Sailor's Children*, also the *Marine Hospital*, which is supported by an emigrant tax of $2 on every cabin passenger, native of a foreign country, and 50 cents for every steerage passenger. The fund from these sources, amounts to nearly $100,000 per annum. There is yet another benevolent marine society, styled *The American Seamen's Friend Society*, whose object is to bring good influences to bear upon this class, by preaching, and by opening boarding-houses, reading-rooms, savings banks, &c.

The Marine Society's office, is at 38 Burling Slip.
St. George's Society of New York, 40 Exchange Place.
St. Andrew's Society, 90 Broadway.
St. David's " 93 Canal street.
St. Nicholas " 11 Wall street.
New England " Astor House.
Italian Benevolent Society, 685 Broadway.
Irish Emigrant " 51 Chambers street.
Hibernian Benevolent Society, 42 Prince street.
German Society of New York, 5 Battery Place.
Hebrew Benevolent Society, 3d. Av. and E. 77th. St.
German Mutual Society, 136 Canal street.
Friendly Sons of St. Patrick, 9 Warren street.

The respective addresses of Societies not given in this list, are to be found in the New York Directory.

THE NEW YORK TURKISH BATH ESTABLISHMENT.

This institution is situated on Laight street, occupying No. 13—only one door from St. John's Park, within a step of Canal street, and only a short distance from Broadway. The cars on Sixth, Seventh, Eighth, and Ninth Avenues pass within a few doors of it. Since it was opened in February, 1865, it has constantly been thronged with bathers. The necessity of Turkish Baths in New York has long been apparent. In England their merits are recognized, and they are held in high esteem by the medical profession and the public, as an important agent in the treatment of many diseases, and as a valuable means of preserving the health. All who visit New York will find it well worth their time to make the Institution a visit. The process of the bath is very interesting, and most people are doubtless familiar with it by the writings of Oriental travellers.

LITERARY & SCIENTIFIC INSTITUTIONS.

THE ASTOR LIBRARY,

Situated on Lafayette Place, near Astor Place, is justly regarded as *the* library collection of the continent. Its literary treasures comprise some of the rarest and most valuable productions of art extant. Dr. Cogswell, the learned Librarian, has collected from all parts of the old world a vast accumulation of costly works in all departments of human knowledge; including about 1000 bibliographical books, and numerous superbly illustrated works of great rarity and value, on almost all subjects—science, history, biography, philology, &c., &c. It already contains nearly 100,000 volumes, and further additions are constantly being made to this collection, by the munificence of its founder, John Jacob Astor who endowed it with the sum of $400,000.

THE NEW YORK TURKISH BATH ESTABLISHMENT

DRS. MILLER, WOOD & CO., Proprietors. Opened February, 1865.

This stately edifice, built of brick, ornamented with brown stone, is of the Romanesque style, and of great symmetrical beauty. Its interior, however, is much more imposing. The entrance to the Library Hall is by a flight of 38 marble steps leading to the second story. This splendid hall is richly decorated with 14 piers finished in imitation of Italian marble, and over these are galleries ranged on either side, inclosed with gilt iron railings. These upper galleries are reached by eight spiral stairways. The height of the Library is near 50 feet, and in the centre of the ceiling is a large skylight, measuring 54 feet by 14, and at each side smaller lights; there are no other windows, these however afford sufficient light for the building. In the east end are inclosures railed in, and the Librarian's rooms. In the lower, or first floor, are the Lecture room and Reading rooms. The floors are of mosaic work. A visit to this noble institution, with its rich and rare collection of sumptuous books, will become a necessity to all who have any love for literature and art.

In the year 1857, William B. Astor, Esq., made a donation, to the Trustees, of the adjoining lot; upon which another structure, in all respects corresponding with the first, has just been erected. Thus the Astor Library has now doubled its proportions—forming the most imposing architectural edifice of its class in the United States. This new building was opened to the public in the Autumn of 1859—immediately after the return of Dr. Cogswell from Europe with a further collection of literary spoils.

THE COOPER UNION

Is a noble building erected by Mr. Peter Cooper, of New York, and is devoted to the "moral, intellectual, and physical improvement of his countrymen." The building covers an entire block, having a front on Third Avenue of 195 feet, on Fourth Avenue 155, on Eighth street 143, and on Seventh street 86. It is in the immediate vicinity of the new "Bible House," the "Astor

Library," the "Mercantile Library," and the rooms of various literary and scientific societies. In the basement is a large lecture-room, 125 feet long by 85 wide and 21 high; and this, and also the first and second stories, which are arranged for stores and offices, are rented, so as to produce a revenue to meet the annual expenses of the "Institute." The "Institute" proper—or the "Union"—commences with the third story, in which is an "exhibition-room," 30 feet high and 125 by 82, lighted from above by a dome. The fourth story may be considered as a part of the third, being a continuation of galleries with alcoves for painting and sculpture. In the fifth story are two large lecture-rooms; and the library, consisting of five rooms, which connect with each other and with the lecture-rooms. There are also rooms for experiments, for instruments, and for the use of artists. The cost of the building is about $300,000, and the annual income from the rented parts is from $25,000 to $30,000. The whole is under the control of a Board of Directors for the benefit of the public; the course of lectures, the library, and the reading-rooms being all free. In the munificence both of the gift and the endowment, the "COOPER INSTITUTE" stands as a monument to its noble-hearted founder more enduring than the pyramids. The School of Design for women has rooms in this building.

THE FREE ACADEMY,

In Twenty-third street, corner of Lexington Avenue, was established in 1848, by the Board of Education of the city of New York, in pursuance of an act passed May 7, 1847, for the purpose of providing higher education for such pupils of the Common Schools as may wish to avail themselves thereof. The Free Academy is under the general superintendence of the Board of Education; but it is specially under the supervision of an Executive Committee, for its care, government, and management, appointed by the Board. All its expenses

Cooper Union.

for instruction, apparatus, library, cabinet collections, books, and stationery, are paid out of the public treasury.

The cost of the ground was $37,810, the edifice, $75,000, and the interior furniture, apparatus, &c., $26,867. The building measures 125 feet by 80, and will accommodate 1000 pupils.

The students are admitted in annual classes, and the full course of study embraces five years.

The Board of Education is authorized by law to confer the usual collegiate degrees on the recommendation of the faculty.

Graduates may become "Resident Graduates," and continue their studies at option. The Academical studies during Term time, continue daily (except Saturday and Sunday) from a quarter before 9 o'clock A. M. to 3 o'clock P. M.

MERCANTILE LIBRARY ASSOCIATION

Occupy the Clinton Hall building in Astor Place, Eighth street. This noble establishment comprises a fine library, reading-room, and lecture-room, also cabinets of minerals, &c. Its literary collections numbering between 40 and 50,000 volumes, in the several departments of general knowledge, including also a valuable series of periodical works, unsurpassed by any other institution. The number of its members at the present time exceeds 4000. This institution, originally established for the use of clerks, has been since thrown open to the public on payment of the subscription, $5 per annum. Clerks pay $1 initiation fee, and $2 subscription.

THE NEW YORK SOCIETY LIBRARY

Is situated in University Place, near Twelfth street. This time-honored institution, founded in 1754, possesses a fine collection of books in general literature, numbering about 38,000 volumes. Permanent members of this institution, by the payment of $25, and the annual fee of $6, become stockholders. Temporary members are admitted on the payment of $10 per annum. To all these literary establishments, visitors are admitted.

THE CITY LIBRARY

Is in the City Hall, and is free to all persons.

THE NEW YORK LAW INSTITUTE

Have a valuable library of law books at No. 41 Chambers street. Open daily.

THE PRINTERS' FREE LIBRARY,

Located at No. 3 Chambers street, has over 4000 volumes. It is open every Saturday evening.

THE WOMAN'S LIBRARY

Is in the New York University Building, fronting on Washington Square.

THE LYCEUM OF NATURAL HISTORY

Is a society of scientific men, formed for the study of natural history. Its rooms are in Fourteenth street, near the 4th Avenue. It possesses a good library, and a large museum of minerals, plants, and specimens of natural history. It is accessible to the public.

THE APPRENTICE'S LIBRARY,

containing about 16,000 volumes for the use of youthful apprentices, is in the Mechanics' Hall, 472 Broadway, near Grand street.

THE MECHANICS' INSTITUTE,

No. 20 Fourth Avenue, has a collection of upwards of 3000 volumes. There is a school attached for the education of the children of mechanics.

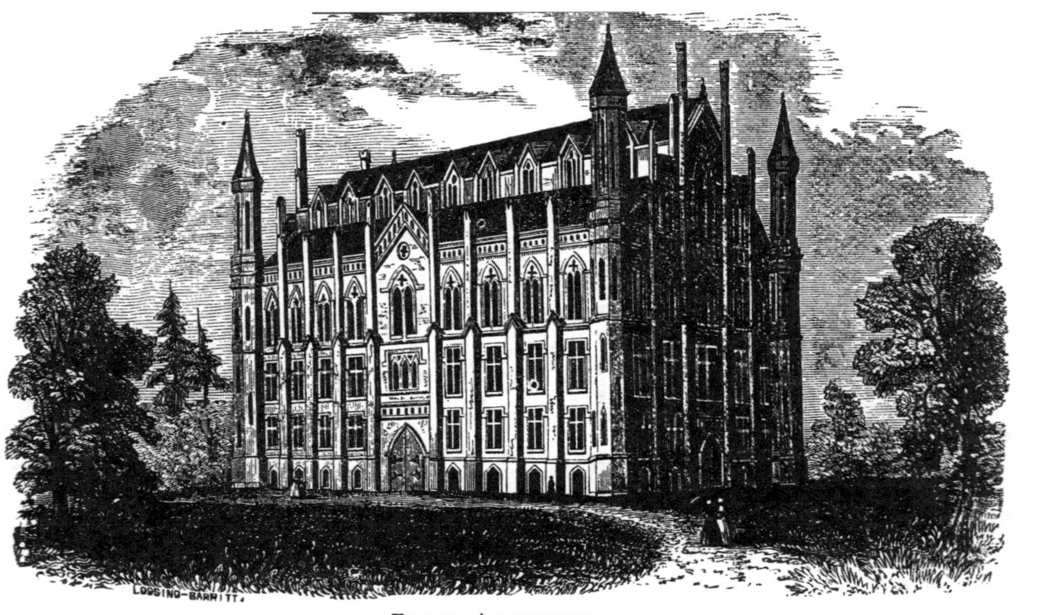

FREE ACADEMY.

THE NEW YORK HISTORICAL SOCIETY,

Established upwards of half a century, have a noble edifice on the corner of Eleventh street and Second Avenue. It is an elegant fire-proof structure, built of yellow sandstone from the province of New Brunswick, and is splendidly fitted up. Its literary collections consist of rare and valuable books pertaining to the history and antiquities of the country; also medals, coins, maps, engravings, &c. The Library comprises about 20,000 volumes. There is a fine Picture-gallery in the uppermost story; the Library Hall, Lecture-room, and various offices are characterized by great architectural beauty. Recently there have been added a fine collection of Nineveh Marbles, presented by James Lenox, Esq., and Dr. Abbott's Egyptian Collection (obtained by liberal subscription), one of the most valuable museums of Egyptian antiquities in the world. The meetings of the society are held on the first Tuesday of each month; there are also occasional Lectures given, in addition to the regular series. Hon. Luther Bradish is the President, and the membership of the association numbers about 1500, including the leading literary men of the country.

AMERICAN ETHNOLOGICAL SOCIETY,

Founded in 1842. The first President of this society was the late Albert Gallatin, formerly Secretary of the Treasury, &c., who held the office until his death in 1849. The object of the society is "the prosecution of inquiries into the origin, progress, and characteristics of the various races of men." This society has collected a large amount of materials, and has published three volumes of Transactions. The meetings are held at the houses of members, on the second Tuesday in each month.

THE NEW YORK JUVENILE ASYLUM,

A fine stone edifice, situated near High Bridge, is a home and reformatory for neglected children. The asylum, by its charter, becomes the legal guardian of all such children as may be committed to it by the voluntary act of their parents or by the precept of a police magistrate. The institution owes its origin to Dr. J. D. Russ of this city, so favorably known for his exertions in establishing the New York Institution for the Blind. The success of the institution has been largely promoted by A. R. Wetmore, Esq., who has been its president and financier almost from its organization. It occupies about 20 acres of ground, which is in part cultivated by the children, who, during their stay in the asylum, are instructed in all the branches of a common school education. As soon as their improvement will warrant their removal, they are sent to the Great West and indentured, where, in a few years, instead of being drawn into the vortex of crime as they almost inevitably would have been if left unprotected in our streets, they will many of them become our law-makers and occupy places of trust. The institution has a *House of Reception* for 200 children, at No. 71 West Thirteenth street. All children, when first committed, must remain in this house ten days, to afford their parents an opportunity of reclaiming them. The two buildings can accommodate about 700. Take Hudson River railroad or Manhattanville stages to Fort Washington or High Bridge.

YOUNG MEN'S CHRISTIAN ASSOCIATION.

This society have rooms in the Bible House, corner of Third Avenue and Ninth street. The Association has a reading-room which is entirely distinct from the library and department for committee and other meetings. Devotional services are held on Wednesday and Saturday evenings. Young men, strangers, and the public are cordially invited.

THE AMERICAN INSTITUTE,

At Cooper Union, has also a select library of works, principally relating to the inventive and mechanic arts. Under the auspices of this association have been held the annual fairs for the purpose of exhibiting the progress of new inventions in science and art.

THE AMERICAN GEOGRAPHICAL AND STATISTICAL SOCIETY

Of New York, hold their monthly meetings at the Historical Society's rooms, in Second Avenue.

THE NEW YORK UNIVERSITY

Is located on the east side of Washington Square, and forms a noble architectural ornament, being of the English collegiate style of architecture. The University was established in 1831, and has ever maintained its high reputation. It has a chancellor, and a corps of professors in the various departments of learning. There is also a grammar school connected with the institution; also a valuable library, philosophical apparatus, &c. The edifice is of marble, and measures about 200 feet in front by 100 in depth: it presents a very beautiful appearance as seen through the thick foliage of the park. The great central gothic window lights the chapel of the University; divine service is held here every Sunday at the usual hours. The principal entrance is by the centre door, up a flight of marble steps. In the upper parts of the building are several chambers and offices, occupied by various societies, literary persons, and artists.

COLUMBIA COLLEGE,

Originally chartered by George II., in 1754, under the title of King's College, till within a short period, stood in Park Place. The present edifice is on Forty-ninth street, near the Fifth Avenue. It has a president and 12 professors; a choice library of rare classical works of about 18,000 volumes, museum, &c. A grammar school is attached to the institution, over which a professor presides as rector.

PUBLIC AND WARD SCHOOLS.

By the report of the Board of Education, we find that there are in New York city, 275 ward schools, including 19 for colored children, evening schools, normal and primary schools. The average annual cost of sustaining these free institutions of popular instruction, amounts to over one million;—which sum is raised for the most part by taxation, and the balance being derived from the State appropriation. The whole number taught in the schools during the year, was over 150,000, including about 3,000 colored children. This estimate, however, comprehends about 10,000 belonging to the various benevolent institutions, the Orphan Asylum, House of Industry, and several others, as well as the Free Academy.

The rooms of the Board of Education are located on the corner of Grand and Elm streets.

WARD SCHOOL, No. 44,

On the corner of North Moore and Varick streets, is a fair specimen of school architecture in the city; being one of the most beautiful and commodious school edifices in the city.

Bible House.

THE NEW BIBLE HOUSE,

Which is approached from Broadway through Astor Place, occupies three fourths of an acre of ground, bounded by Third and Fourth Avenues, and Eighth and Ninth streets. The form of this gigantic edifice is nearly triangular. It has a front of 198 feet on Fourth Avenue, 202 on Eighth street, 96 on Third Avenue, and 232 on Ninth street. Its average depth is about 50 feet. It is the property of the American Bible Society. This imposing-looking edifice, which is substantially built of brick, with stone facings, cost nearly $300,000. The principal entrance, which is on the Fourth Avenue, has four columns, surmounted with cornice. In the fourth story is a stone figure representing Religion holding a Bible.

The receipts of the Society, at the first year of its organization in 1816–17, were $37,779.35; its receipts since then amount to about $5,000,000. It has put in circulation about nine millions of Bibles and Testaments; and given some $500,000 to various Missionary Stations to aid in the publications of the Holy Scriptures. It has supplied thousands of seamen and criminals with copies; as well as distributed hundreds of thousands to private families, hotels, &c., in every part of the United States. It has produced editions of the Bible, or portions of it, in about 24 different dialects, and aided in issuing it in others. In this spacious building the following Societies have their Rooms, viz: the Protestant Episcopal Society for the Promotion of Evangelical Knowledge, the American Board of Commissioners for Foreign Missions, the American Home Missionary Society, the New York Colonization Society, Society for the Amelioration of the Condition of the Jews, the House of Refuge, Children's Aid Society, Home of the Friendless. Nearly 600 persons are employed in the Bible House when in full operation.

COLLEGE OF ST. FRANCIS XAVIER.

This institution, situated on Fifteenth street, between Fifth and Sixth Avenues, was founded in 1850, and incorporated as a University in 186*. With its Grammar School it contains about four hundred pupils. The library contains about 15,000 volumes. The Rev. Joseph Loyzance is president.

MANHATTAN COLLEGE.

This newly incorporated University is situated at Manhattanville.

THEOLOGICAL INSTITUTIONS.

THE UNION THEOLOGICAL SEMINARY

Is situated No. 9 University Place, between Waverley Place and Eighth street. The principal edifice comprises four large lecture rooms, a chapel, library of 16,000 volumes, and studies, also other rooms for students. It has 6 professors, and usually about 100 students. It was founded in 1836.

THE GENERAL THEOLOGICAL SEMINARY

Of the Episcopal Church is situated in Twentieth street, corner of Ninth Avenue, near the Hudson, two miles from the City Hall. There are two handsome buildings of stone, for the accommodation of professors and students. The Board of Trustees consists of all the bishops, and one trustee from each diocese in the United States. The institution is well endowed and in a flourishing condition.

PICTURE GALLERIES, &c.

THE ARTISTS' STUDIO BUILDING

Is a fine brick edifice in Tenth street, near the Sixth Avenue, and occupied by artists, &c.

THE NATIONAL ACADEMY OF DESIGN.

The new building for the National Academy of Design is one of the most remarkable structures in the city. Principally so, because it is the most prominent example thus far set before the public, of the effort now being made to revive the Gothic Architecture of the Thirteenth Century in its true spirit, and adapt it to our own circumstances, materials, and necessities. The public have, unfortunately, been led to call it Venetian Gothic; and, from its similarity in proportion, and the fact that the upper story is decorated with diagonal lines of color introduced into the wall itself, and has no windows, that it is a copy of the famous Ducal Palace. But a careful examination, in comparison with a good photograph of that building, will dispel the delusion.

The carvings on the capitals of the first and second stories are well worthy of careful examination, and are more particularly remarkable from the fact that they are almost entirely designed by the men who carved them, and are the result of careful study from natural leaves and flowers. The work of the architect, in connection with this decorative work, consisted principally of instructions given to the workmen in the art of design applied to their own work.

The fronts of the building are built of white Westchester county marble, banded with grey-wacke. The ornamental iron work of the exterior is worthy of careful attention, being entirely wrought out on the anvil. The main entrance-gates are wonderful for their lightness, careful finish, and strength, being the most elaborate piece of architectural wrought-iron in this country.

The building is finished throughout with white pine, ash, mahogany, oak, and black walnut,—no paint being used, but all the woods showing their natural grain.

The grand staircase approaching the galleries is of solid oak, trimmed with walnut, finished in wood on the under as well as upper sides.

The interior accommodations consist as follows: On

the first floor are the janitor's apartments and the schools, with their appropriate dressing rooms. On the second story are the reading-room, libraries, council-room, and lecture-room, together with necessary retiring rooms and an office for business. On the third story are the grand central hall, four picture galleries, and the sculpture-room. This edifice has been erected at a cost of about $150,000, under the superintendence of the architect, P. B. Wright, Esq., of this city.

The annual exhibitions of the Academy are held during the months of April, May, June, and July, during which the building is open to the public for a small admission fee. The works of living artists only are exhibited, and no pictures are accepted that have been previously exhibited in New York.

The exhibition of the Artists' Fund Society is generally held in the galleries of the Academy, and takes place in November and December, annually. It is a noble charity, devoted to the relief of sick and poor artists.

THE INSTITUTE OF FINE ARTS

Is situated at 625 Broadway. This is a fine collection of paintings and statuary.

THE NEW YORK PRESS.

There are about fifteen daily papers published in New York, with an aggregate circulation of 140,000 copies. About two thirds of this number are distributed in the city, the balance are sent by mail to various parts of the country. Most of the offices are accessible to public inspection during the hours of 2 to 4 o'clock.

THE TIMES OFFICE

Is situated at the end of Park Row, facing Chatham street. It is an attractive architectural ornament to this active centre of the printing business. In the vicinity are the N. Y. Tribune office, the Tract Society, the Sunday Times, the Sunday Courier, the Mercury, and other papers. On the Nassau side of the Times building are the Observer, Scientific American, the Century, the United States Journal, &c. On this account this site has been recently styled "Printing House Square."

The New York Times building, erected during the panic year, and first occupied on the first day of May, 1858, is a noble structure, constructed of stone and iron, and perfectly fireproof; five stories in height; the walls a light olive-colored stone, brought from Nova Scotia. Complete in all its appointments, this building deserves especial mention, if for no other reason than that it is the only newspaper office in the United States which combines within itself the requisites of thorough fitness and the elegance of refined taste. Our readers, we are assured, will be interested in a description of the parts of this establishment.

The site is that which was for many years occupied by the Old Brick Church (the Rev. Dr. Spring's), an ancient place of worship, erected at the period when green fields adorned the space now densely crowded with great warehouses, stores, and banks; when honest old Knickerbockers held the site of the Park to be a journey out of town; and where the bones of early residents of the city were solemnly laid in earth that is now undermined by lighted vaults and rendered vocal by the ceaseless clash of ponderous machinery.

Thus much for the exterior. We descend into the spacious vaults which run down and out towards the centre of the square. The peculiar fitness of the location for the purposes of a newspaper establishment is here displayed in perfection. No daily paper of circulation so large as that of the Times (40,000) can dispense with the use of Hoe's lightning press. That magnificent piece of machinery is necessarily bulky, and requires ample space. The press-room vaults of the Times are of extraordinary dimensions, extending around the three fronts of the building, and having the following measurements: On Spruce street, one hundred by twenty-six feet; on Park row, one hundred by twenty feet; on Nassau street, ninety-five by fifteen feet, with a uniform depth of twenty-four feet below the curb. These vaults are far the finest ever constructed in New York.

On the Nassau street or easterly side are the steam boilers and engine; on the northerly side, two immense power-presses, of Hoe's manufacture, one ten-cylinder and one six-cylinder, are placed. On the Park row side are the folding and mailing rooms and the storerooms for paper—the latter opening to the pavement above by means of a huge movable vault-light, which admits of the passage of the largest reams of paper required in printing. The vaults are admirably lighted, and an excellent ventilation is sustained.

The various editorial, composing, and other offices of the establishment are upon a most extended scale. The cost of the edifice and ground, amounted to something less than $300,000.

The Herald Office and vaults, as well as those of the *Tribune*, are also of similar gigantic proportions. The *Sun*, in Fulton street, at the corner of Nassau street, has also immense vaults. The *Evening Post* is issued from the corner of Nassau and Liberty streets.

PLACES OF AMUSEMENT.

THE NEW BOWERY THEATRE,

Situated on the Bowery, near Hester street, is one of the finest edifices of its kind in this country. It is capable of accommodating 6,000 people, and is estimated to have cost $80,000.

WALLACK'S THEATRE,

on Broadway, corner of Thirteenth street, is a well-conducted theatre. It is usually successful in its entertainments.

OLYMPIC THEATRE.

No. 622 Broadway, is another fashionable resort, as is also

NIBLO'S GARDEN,

The entrance to which is under the Metropolitan Hotel.

THE WINTER GARDEN,

Formerly the Metropolitan Theatre, is on Broadway, opposite Bond street. The interior arrangement is admirable, as a good view of the stage can be had from any part of the house.

THE BOWERY THEATRE,

Situated in the Bowery, near Canal street, occupies the site upon which three theatres have been successively burnt and rebuilt. The present edifice is of the Doric order of architecture. This place of entertainment is usually celebrated for spectacle and the broader kind of humor.

BARNUM'S AMERICAN MUSEUM,

Founded 1810, is at the corner of Broadway and Ann street, contains several large halls, 100 feet in length, filled with curiosities of every description: besides numerous paintings, a mineralogical collection, and other objects of interest.

THE EGYPTIAN MUSEUM

Is located in the New York Historical Society Building. It contains several hundred relics, collected with great care and industry by the learned Dr. Abbott, during a residence of twenty years on the banks of the Nile. Here are to be seen mummied men and quadrupeds, the slates of the school-boys in Pharaoh's time, and the remains of the lamps that were used to lighten the darkness of Egypt. Many of the objects here are three thousand years old.

THE NEW YORK STADT THEATRE,

In the Bowery, nearly opposite the Bowery Theatre, is a German Opera House, and has a well-selected company.

THE ACADEMY OF MUSIC,

On the corner of Irving Place and Fourteenth street, is the largest theatre in New York, and the most elegant in its appointments. It occupies an area of 24,000 square feet. The theatre measures 121 feet by 114, and will seat about 4000 persons. The several tiers of

Metropolitan Hotel.

boxes are beautifully decorated with gilt ornaments and chandeliers: and the dome is richly painted in panels, representing Music, Poetry, Comedy, and Tragedy. The building is well constructed for sound, and in its various appointments admirably adapted as a place of popular amusement. The cost of the ground and building is estimated at $350,000.

BRYANT'S MINSTRELS,

No. 472 Broadway, is one of the best of places "to wile away an hour." It was in this hall that Ethiopian Minstrelsy first found "a local habitation and a name." The place is well worthy of a visit.

CARMEN.

The prices authorized by law for carmen, for ordinary loads, within the distance of half a mile, is 50 cents; if over that, and within a mile, one third more may be charged; for any greater distance, in the same proportion. If a carman charges beyond the legal rates, he cannot collect any thing for his services; but he is not obliged to deliver goods conveyed by him until his legal charge be paid. Every carman is required to have his number distinctly marked on his cart.

HOTELS.

New York is justly distinguished for the number and magnificence of its hotels. On the line of Broadway there are upwards of 25 of these stately and capacious buildings. In other parts of the city they no less abound, although less costly in their appointments. It will be necessary to detail the more important of these hotels separately.

THE ASTOR HOUSE,

The first colossal edifice of its class, was built over 20 years ago, of solid granite, and although so many others have arisen since, this well-appointed and extensive establishment still retains its high position. It is capable of accommodating 600 guests.

Several of the hotels are conducted upon the European plan—the guests hiring their rooms, with or without board. Of these we might mention

THE INTERNATIONAL HOTEL,

The first floor and basements of which are occupied by Taylor's world-renowned saloons, and which form one of the greatest objects of interest to the stranger, there being nothing in the world comparable to them, from five to ten thousand persons taking refreshments daily. The hotel building was erected some seven years since, at a cost of over $500,000. It should be seen by all strangers.

MOORE'S MADISON SQUARE HOTEL,

Corner of Twenty-first street and Broadway. Well arranged for families and transient company. J. L. Moore, proprietor.

THE METROPOLITAN HOTEL,

Situated on Broadway, corner of Prince street, is built of brown stone, and is six stories in height. The cost of this building and ground was upwards of $800,000. It is furnished throughout in the most splendid and

St. Denis Hotel.

costly style, having all the accommodations and conveniences that the most luxurious taste could devise. The entire establishment is heated by steam, and has a ventilating process. The cost of the interior decorations and furniture has been estimated at about $200,000; making the whole investment in this superb establishment, one million of dollars. It is stated that the water and gas pipes, which are carried throughout all the apartments of this mammoth hotel, measure 12 miles; and there are 13,000 yards of carpeting spread over its 400 or 500 rooms, which, with the superb drapery, cost $40,000; the furniture, $50,000; the mirrors (including some of the largest ever imported), $18,000; the silverware, $14,000—not to mention other items.

THE ST. NICHOLAS,

Occupying about 300 feet on Broadway, corner of Spring st., stands a monument of architectural beauty, of the Corinthian order and of marble. The immense *façade*, six stories high, is of surpassing elegance. It was erected in 1854, at a cost of over a million of dollars. Within the portico of the main entrance, supported by four Corinthian pillars with rich capitals, the spectator looks down a columned vista two hundred feet in length and averaging sixty feet in width. The upper part of the house, reached by a massive staircase of polished oak, is divided into three sections communicating by corridors, and contains *six hundred rooms.* On the second and third floors are one hundred suites of apartments. The three largest dining-rooms comfortably accommodate six hundred guests. The public rooms and chambers are decorated and furnished in the most sumptuous style, while the immense corridors are carpeted entire with the richest tapestry fabrics, rendering the step inaudible, and lighted by magnificent chandeliers and candelabras placed at short intervals throughout their whole extent. The fourth, fifth, and sixth floors are devoted to private parlors, chambers, and single rooms. The original disbursement for mirrors amounted to $40,000, and the service of silver ware and Sheffield plate cost $50,000. Whatever ornament wealth could purchase or skill produce has been lavished upon this palatial structure, in which one thousand guests may enjoy all of the comforts and luxuries of life.

From the telegraph office in the bar-room, messages may be transmitted to almost any part of the Union. More than three hundred waiters are in attendance. The hotel is lighted by gas. The daily expenses of the St. Nicholas are $1,500. As a security against fire the entire establishment can be deluged with water in five minutes.

THE PRESCOTT HOUSE

Occupies the opposite corner of Spring street, being Nos. 529 and 531 Broadway. The hotel was so named in honor of the celebrated American historian. It is built of brick with quaintly wrought stone work about the windows. The spacious triple-columned and highly ornamented entrance hall is one of the finest in the country.

Except in magnitude, this hotel building is of surpassing beauty. The ceilings are elaborately panelled, carved, and profusely adorned with gilding. The floors of the principal rooms and halls are covered with tiles of various rich colors, arranged in a carpet-like pattern, which contrast beautifully with the white and gold of the walls and ceiling. A considerable part of the furniture of the Prescott House was made to order in Paris and London.

THE CLARENDON

Is another elegant establishment on the corner of Fourth Avenue and Eighteenth street, in the vicinity of Union and Gramercy Park. This hotel is divided into suites of apartments, with all the modern improvements and adornments of taste. It is of the Elizabethan order of architecture, and cost $80,000.

GRAMERCY PARK HOUSE.

HOFFMAN HOUSE.

BRANDRETH HOUSE,

Corner of Broadway, Canal, and Lispenard Streets, is located in the most central part of Broadway, and all parts of the city can be reached by city cars and omnibuses constantly passing the door. The rooms are elegantly furnished—many of them in suites of communicating parlors and chambers, suitable for families and parties travelling together. Being kept on the European plan, guests may live in the most economical or luxurious manner. Meals served at all hours at the shortest notice. The attention of merchants visiting the city is particularly called to this hotel, as it is situated on Broadway, in the very centre of the wholesale, jobbing, and retail business of New York, and can be reached by omnibus or city cars from all the steamboat landings and railway depots. Wm. J. Kerr, Proprietor.

GRAMERCY PARK HOUSE,

Is another first-class edifice, of colossal proportions, between 20th and 21st streets, facing the delightful shrubbery of a beautiful inclosure called Gramercy Park, from whence the house derives its name. This is one of the largest hotels in the city, built of substantial brown stone, and in one of the most aristocratic localities of Gotham. In its internal arrangements it is unsurpassed, and contains spacious accommodations for six to eight hundred guests. Those who may be so fortunate as to select this hotel during their residence in the city, will find its kind and courteous proprietors, Messrs. Judson & Ely, ever ready to contribute to their comfort and enjoyment.

HOFFMAN HOUSE,

Is another elegant establishment on the corner of Broadway and 25th street, and opposite Madison Square. This hotel is one of the most beautiful in the city, and none who visit New York should fail to see it. It is built of white marble, and conducted on the European plan. It has a capacity for about 350 guests, with superior accommodations, and is extensively patronized by the "Upper Ten." Its situation is in a delightful part of the city, and is a central location for all of the Eastern and Northern railroads, and forms a most eligible and convenient stopping-place for travellers, while the cool and delightful square opposite forms an attractive feature to all.

BANCROFT HOUSE,

Corner of Broadway and 20th street. By a glance at the city map, it will be seen that the central locality of this large and pleasant hotel secures ready communication, by railroad and stage, with all the most desirable parts of the city—from the Battery to Central Park. This entire establishment has lately been thoroughly renovated throughout, and furnished with accommodations that cannot fail of giving satisfaction to the most fastidious.

THE BELVIDERE HOUSE,

Occupies the southeast corner of 14th street and Fourth avenue, opposite Union Square and the celebrated Washington Monument. This is a quiet, neat house, on the European plan, and the restaurant connected with the establishment is abundantly supplied with the best the market affords. The situation is in one of the most delightful parts of the city, and the house is well patronized by the aristocratic families of both town and country.

UNION SQUARE HOTEL,

Corner 15th street and Union Square, A. J. Dam, proprietor. The location of this house is one of the most pleasant in the city. Fine suites of rooms, handsomely furnished, for the accommodation of transient as well as permanent boarders. This house is kept on the old plan of the regular *table d' hôte*, and connected with it is a first-class restaurant.

IRVING HOUSE,

Is a first-class hotel, conducted on the European plan, at the corner of Broadway and 12th street. Accommodations for families or transient guests. The location is unsurpassed, being in the immediate vicinity of A. T. Stewart's new store, Wallack's Theatre, etc., and near the Union Square. Geo. W. Hunt, Proprietor.

HOTEL DIEZ, LATE PRESCOTT HOUSE,

dway, cor. Spring St. FREDERICK DIEZ, Proprietor

ST. DENIS HOTEL.

Opposite Grace Church, and only three blocks below Union Square and the Academy of Music, is the *St. Denis Hotel.* It is architecturally one of the handsomest buildings on Broadway, occupying seventy-six feet on that thoroughfare, and one hundred and twenty on Eleventh street. Besides parlors, reception-rooms, and reading-rooms, the St. Denis contains over one hundred and fifty well lighted and ventilated apartments. The hotel is kept on the European plan, and like the Prescott is the frequent resort of wealthy and distinguished foreigners. The "up town" location of the St. Denis is on the most fashionable part of Broadway.

THE EVERETT HOUSE,

Located on the north side of Union Square and Seventeenth street, from its position is, like the Clarendon, a convenient and delightful place for visitors, being not only in the fashionable part of the city, but also con tiguous to the cars, stages, &c.

THE LA FARGE HOUSE,

In Broadway, facing Bond street, is a magnificent structure, with a frontage of 200 feet, seven stories high, and built of marble, it was completed in 1856; its estimated cost being $250,000. Its interior arrangements are parallel with those of the other magnificent establishments on Broadway, and like them, is usually much resorted to by visitors. Like the Prescott House, it is capable of accommodating 400 guests.

THE NEW YORK HOTEL,

Broadway, extending from Washington to Waverley Place, is another large and fashionable house, and admirable in all its departments.

THE BREVOORT HOUSE,

On the Fifth Avenue, corner of Eighth street, is a noble and spacious Hotel, fitted up in elegant style, and being on the great avenue of fashion, commands a fine view of the *beau monde.*

THE NEW FIFTH AVENUE HOTEL,

Under the control of Col. Stevens, is an object of special note. In addition to its beautiful site—being opposite to the shrubbery of Madison Square—it stretches its façades of white marble down Twenty-third and Twenty-fourth streets, both equally known as among the most aristocratic of our thoroughfares. In its internal arrangements, it is unsurpassed—furnishing entire accommodation for eight hundred guests, and containing more than one hundred suites of apartments, each combining the conveniences and luxury of parlor, chamber, dressing, and bathing rooms. All the rooms, besides being well lighted and ventilated, will have means of access by a perpendicular railway—intersecting each story—in addition to the broad and capacious corridors and stairways, independent of the ordinarv and usual approaches from floor to floor.

As to location, this hotel is much nearer the termini of the Eastern and Northern Railroads than others further down town, and from the evidence of the march of improvement, it must continue to be the centre of civilization for many years to come. It will be the most eligible for Southerners, not only as a transient stopping-place *en route*, but as a delightful home during those periods devoted to summer recreation.

THE ALBEMARLE,

Another very elegant hotel, is situated at the corner of Broadway and 24th street.

Fifth Avenue Hotel.

THE CHURCHES OF NEW YORK.

It is estimated that there are about 300 churches in New York; many of them being of great elegance. We annex brief notices of the more prominent and noteworthy.

TRINITY CHURCH.

Fronting Wall street, with its portals invitingly open every day in the year, stands Trinity Church, a beautiful temple of worship, in strange contiguity with the busy marts where "merchants most do congregate." It is the third edifice of the kind erected upon the spot, the first having been destroyed in the great fire of 1776. This fine gothic structure was completed in 1846, having been seven years in building, under the careful superintendence of Mr. Upjohn, the architect. The church is 192 feet in length, 80 in breadth, and 60 in height. The interior will richly repay examination. Among many relics there carefully preserved, is an elaborate chancel service of silver, presented to the corporation by Queen Anne.

The steeple towers up 284 feet in height; the walls of the church are nearly 50 feet high, and the whole edifice, both as to its exterior and interior, is regarded by most persons as the most elegant and cathedral-like of the churches of the city. Do not forget to ascend the steeple to get a panoramic view of the city.

The grave-yard of Old Trinity occupies nearly an entire block. Within it are the venerated tombs of Alexander Hamilton, the statesman and friend of Washington; the heroic commander Lawrence, and many other illustrious public men.

Adjoining Trinity buildings, and a few feet from Broadway, stands the monumental tribute of the Corporation of Trinity Church to the honored "Sugar House Martyrs." Of finely cut and ornamented brown stone, it presents a graceful appearance, while it attracts the especial interest of every American patriot from the fact, that the ground immediately under and around it, is rich with the ashes of our Revolutionary fathers.

ST. PAUL'S CHAPEL,

The third Episcopal church established in the city, was erected in 1766. It stands between Fulton and Vesey streets, opposite Barnum's Museum. The length of the edifice is 151 feet, and the width 73 feet. The steeple is 203 feet high.

On the front, in a niche of red sandstone, in the centre of a large pediment supported by four Ionic columns, is a white marble statue of St. Paul, leaning on a sword. Also in the front part of the niche there is inserted a slab of white marble, bearing an inscription to the memory of General Montgomery, who fell at Quebec during the Revolution, and whose remains were removed to New York by order of the State in 1818. At the lower side of the church, facing Broadway, is an obelisk of white marble, erected in honor of Thomas Addis Emmet, the Irish patriot and barrister, who died here in 1827. The inscriptions are in Latin, Irish, and English.

ST. JOHN'S CHAPEL

(Episcopal). This is one of the associate churches of the Trinity Corporation. It is located facing St. John's Park, on a line with Varick street. It is not modern in style, but yet a very noble looking edifice. It is built of sandstone, and is very spacious, measuring 132 feet by 80. It has a deep portico in front, formed by a pediment and four massive columns.

Church of the Puritans.

In all the ancient churches of New York city, the plan of a collegiate charge was the rule. The ancient Episcopal church of the city was established on this basis. Trinity church was considered the parish church, and had a collegiate charge; St. George's, St. John's, and St. Paul's were called "Chapels." St. George's is now a distinct charge, but the other two are still collegiate.

ST. MARK'S CHURCH

(Episcopal), situate in Stuyvesant street, to the east of the Bowery, was built in its present form in 1826.

The steeple is lofty, but somewhat venerable in appearance, which is indeed the character of the entire structure. The church is venerable also on account of its historic associations; it stands on what was the estate of Petrus Stuyvesant, the last of the Dutch governors, and his remains rest in a vault under the church, over which, on the east side, is a tablet indicating the fact. Here also repose the mortal remains of the English governor, Col. Sloughter, and those of the American governor, Tompkins. The Rev. Dr. Vinton is the present minister.

ST. GEORGE'S CHURCH

(Episcopal). This spacious and elegant structure, the most capacious ecclesiastical edifice in the city, is situated in East Sixteenth street, opposite Stuyvesant Square. It was erected in 1849, and for architectural beauty is entitled to the first rank among the religious edifices of New York. Its imposing exterior, and vast interior, unsupported by any visible columns, either to roof or gallery, impart to it a fine effect. Its architecture is of the Byzantine order; its length 170 feet by 94 in width. Its entire cost $250,000. The adjoining rectory cost $20,000, and the chapel $10,000. The ground upon which the church stands was given by the late Peter G. Stuyvesant. The Rev. Dr Tyng is rector.

ST. THOMAS' CHURCH

(Episcopal), corner of Houston street and Broadway, one of the early and best specimens of the Gothic, was erected in 1826. Its measurement is 113 by 62 feet; and is built of rough stones. A fire occurred in 1851, which burnt the interior, and to this circumstance is owing its present commodious and elegant internal appointments. Rev. Dr. Morgan is the incumbent.

TRINITY CHAPEL

(Episcopal), situated on Twenty-fifth street, near Broadway, and extending from Twenty-fifth to Twenty-sixth street, is a spacious and elegant edifice, erected by the Trinity Church Corporation, and cost $260,000. The length of the building is 180 feet; width, 54 feet. The inside walls are of Caen stone; the windows are ot richly stained glass, and the ceiling painted blue, with gilt ornaments. The floors are tiled; and the seats are movable benches, as in the cathedrals of the Continent.

GRACE CHURCH

(Episcopal). This superb edifice, the most ornate of the ecclesiastical buildings of New York, is located in Broadway, near Tenth street, and commands a fine view of the great avenue of the city, north and south. The lofty spiral and richly decorated steeple is an object of universal admiration. There is one large and two less sized doors in front. Over the main entrance is a circular window of stained glass, and two tall, oblong windows in each side of the upper section of the tower. Within is a grand array of pillars, carved work, and upwards of forty windows of stained glass, each giving different hues of vision. There is a little too much of theatrical glitter in the interior, to comport with the chastened solemnities of religious worship. It was

CHURCH OF HOLY COMMUNION.

built in 1845. Mr. Renwick was the architect. The cost of the building was $145,000. The Rev. Dr. Taylor is the present rector.

THE FIRST BAPTIST CHURCH,

Corner of Broome and Elizabeth streets, was erected in 1841. It measures 99 by 75 feet, and 70 in height, is of the Gothic order, built of rough stone, with the lintels, cornices, and battlements of brown sandstone. It was constructed during the pastorate of the late Dr. Spencer H. Cone.

THE DUTCH REFORMED CHURCH,

Situate on Fourth street and Lafayette Place, was built in 1839. It measures 110 feet long by 75 wide; it cost $160,000. Its exterior is very good, but its interior is characterized by simple elegance. The pulpit is of white marble. The Collegiate Dutch Church is one of the oldest establishments of the kind in the city. Associated with this Church Association are the "North Church," in Fulton street; the new and elegant Church in Fifth Avenue, corner of Twenty-ninth street; the Ninth Street Church, and that we have just described, on Lafayette Place. The venerable Dr. De Witt and others are the officiating clergymen.

THE DUTCH REFORMED CHURCH,

Situate on the east side of Washington Square, was erected in 1840, of rough granite. It is in the Gothic style, with a large centre window, and two towers. Its interior is very finished and effective, especially the ornamental carved work of the organ, pulpit, &c. The entire cost of the edifice was $125,000. The Rev. Dr. Hutton has long been the minister.

ST. PATRICK'S CATHEDRAL

(Roman Catholic), on the corner of Prince and Mott streets, was erected in 1815. This building, although not of much architectural beauty, is very spacious, it being nearly 160 feet in length by 80 in width. The rear of the church is ornamented with Gothic windows. The interior presents an imposing effect, the ceiling being very lofty, from which spring large pillars, on which are lamps pendant. It will accommodate 2000 persons.

CHURCH OF THE HOLY REDEEMER,

A new German Catholic Church, on Third street, near Avenue A, is a very costly and elegant structure. The spire is 265 feet high, and the edifice is of the Byzantine order. It is a most ornamental church, as to its interior, having richly stained windows, broad aisles, marble columns, lofty roof, richly decorated, and a magnificent altar, with confessionals, &c. It is estimated at over $100,000.

FIRST PRESBYTERIAN CHURCH,

On the Fifth Avenue, between Eleventh and Twelfth streets, is a fine stone building, measuring 119 feet by 80; the height of the tower being 160 feet. It cost $75,000.

THE CONGREGATIONAL CHURCH,

Corner of Thirty-fourth street and Sixth Avenue, is a new and beautiful edifice, very spacious and imposing in its aspect. Its style is Gothic, and the interior decorations are in excellent keeping. The organ-screen and pulpit present exquisite specimens of carved work. The Rev. Dr. Thompson is the minister.

THE PRESBYTERIAN CHURCH,

On Madison Avenue, facing the Square, is another brown stone church, exceedingly neat in style. Rev. Dr. Adams is the minister.

THE BRICK CHURCH

(Presbyterian), situate on the corner of Thirty-seventh street and Fifth Avenue, is a spacious brick edifice, with lofty spire. Rev. Dr. Spring is the minister.

ST. PAUL'S M. E. CHURCH,

On Fourth Avenue, corner of Twenty-second street, is a new magnificent edifice, built of marble, in the Romanesque style. Its entire length is 146 feet, by 77; the height of the spire is 210 feet. The cost of the church, parsonage, &c., is estimated at $130,000.

CHURCH OF THE MESSIAH,

(Unitarian), of which the Rev. Dr. Osgood is minister, is situated on the northwest corner of Madison Avenue and Twenty-eighth street.

THE PRESBYTERIAN CHURCH,

On the junction of Tenth street and University Place, is a neat stone edifice, measuring 116 feet by 65, exclusive of a lecture-room in the rear, 72 feet by 25. There is a fine Gothic window over the principal entrance. The tower is 184 feet in height. The cost of this church was $56,000. Rev. Dr. Potts is the minister.

THE FOURTH UNIVERSALIST CHURCH,

Situated on Broadway, between Spring and Prince streets, extends back to Crosby street, the main building being on the rear of the lot. It is brick, 110 feet long, by 77 wide, and about 70 feet in height. The interior is in the Gothic style, and very elegant. The pulpit and organ are richly carved. The entrance from Broadway is of brown stone. Rev. Dr. Chapin is the minister.

CHURCH OF THE HOLY COMMUNION

(Episcopal), on the corner of Twentieth street and Sixth Avenue, is a singular-looking building of brown stone, in the form of a cross. Its extreme length is 104 feet, by 66 in width. The turret on the south corner is 70 feet in height. The interior is novel and imposing, although divested of ornament. It is, strictly speaking, the only free Episcopal Church of its class, in the upper part of the city. Strangers can enter the church with perfect freedom, and seat themselves in any part of it. There is a great want of other accommodations of this class. Will not some one of our wealthy citizens (while living we should prefer) endow another truly Free Episcopal Church like this? It would be an enduring monument of Christian liberality to such a spirit. Rev. Dr. Muhlenberg is the rector.

FIFTH AVENUE PRESBYTERIAN CHURCH,

On the corner of Nineteenth street and Fifth Avenue, erected in 1853, is another of the elegant religious edifices which adorn the city. Its cost is estimated at nearly $90,000. Rev. Dr. Rice is the minister.

THE FRENCH CHURCH

The congregation of the French Church, styled *Eglise du St. Esprit*, has removed from Franklin street, corner of Church, to 22d street, between Fifth and Sixth Avenues. The new church is Gothic, and very elegant. It will seat about one thousand persons. The rector is the Rev. Dr. Verren.

JEWS' SYNAGOGUES.

There are upwards of a dozen Synagogues in this city. The most notable are the following:

Shaarai Tephila (Gates of Prayer), No. 112 Wooster street, near Prince street, and

Bnai Jeshurun (Sons of Jeshurun), in Greene street, near Houston street.

CALVARY CHURCH

(Episcopal), on the corner of Fourth Avenue and 21st street, was erected in 1847, at the cost of $80,000. It presents a picturesque appearance, being built of brown stone. The interior is very spacious and cathedral-like. Adjoining the church is the rectory, also in the Gothic style.

THE NEW ST. PATRICK'S CATHEDRAL,

On the Fifth Avenue and 50th street, now in process of erection, will, when finished, become the crowning architectural ornament of the city.

THE CHURCH OF THE PURITANS

(Congregational), on Union Square, corner of 15th street, is of white marble, of the later Norman or Lombard style. The Rev. Dr. Cheever is the minister.

CHURCH OF ALL SOULS

(Unitarian), corner of Fourth Avenue and 20th street, is an eccentric and remarkable edifice, being built in the style of the Italian churches of the middle ages, of brick and delicate cream-colored stone in alternate courses. Adjoining the church, on 20th street, is the parsonage. Included in the design is to be a spire, or campanile, 300 feet high. The Rev. Dr. Bellows is the minister.

THE TABERNACLE CHURCH

(Baptist), in Second Avenue, near 10th street, adjoining the Historical Society's building, is another Gothic edifice of much beauty and architectural attraction.

ELEGANT PRIVATE RESIDENCES.

In order to form any adequate idea of the progress and opulence of New York, the visitor should not omit to visit the Fifth Avenue, the great centre of wealth and fashion. In other sections of the city are to be seen numerous costly private mansions, such as Lafayette Place, St. Mark's Place, Washington Square, Gramercy Park, Madison Park, Union Square, and the several streets that intersect the upper portions of the metropolis. Passing into the Fifth Avenue from Washington Square, we meet at the junction of Ninth street a stately edifice, once the residence of the late Henry Brevoort. Diagonally opposite to this, on the corner of 8th street, is the Brevoort House, a first-class family hotel on a large scale. On the corner of Tenth street is a house in the style of a French chateau, the property of Mr. Schiff.

On the corner of 12th street and Fifth Avenue stands the noble mansion of James Lenox. On the southeast corner of 15th street is the superb establishment occupied by Mr. Haight: directly opposite, that of Mr. Benkard. Turning to the corner of 16th street, to the left, may be seen the elegant mansion of Col. Thorne; it will be distinguished by its ample courtyard.

On the right-hand corner of 16th street is the stately mansion of Mr. Lorillard Spencer, which is said to have cost $100,000. At the northeast corner of 18th street may be seen Mr. Belmont's elegant house; and on the northwest corner of 20th street is the residence of R. L. Stuart, Esq. At the northwest corner of 34th street and Fifth Avenue is to be seen perhaps the most sumptuous private mansion in the city—that formerly owned by Dr. Townsend, since purchased by A. T Stewart. The private residence of W. B. Astor, Esq.

on Fifth Avenue and 33d street, is another magnificent edifice. There are numerous other superb buildings that we have not indicated, along the line of this avenue and elsewhere, which deserve a separate notice, but this our limits forbid.

THE ATHENEUM CLUB

Have their rooms at 23 Union Place. It is an association of men of letters, artists, and members of the liberal professions, numbering some 400 to 500, who meet for the purposes of social intercourse, &c. The establishment is elegantly furnished.

THE UNION CLUB,

On corner of Fifth Avenue and 22d street, is one of the most splendid structures in the city. It measures about 50 feet by 100, is built in superb style of brown stone, and cost about $300,000.

THE NEW YORK CHESS CLUB

Have their rooms in the N. Y. University. It numbers about 80 members. Initiation fee, $5. Subscription, $10 per annum.

THE CENTURY CLUB

Have their rooms at 42 East 15th street.

THE SKETCH CLUB,

Of New York, hold their meetings in the University buildings.

NOTABLE STORES, ETC.

The stores of New York, being celebrated alike for the beauty of their architecture and variety of their stock, claim our special notice. Starting from down town, at No. 75 John street, we find the well known house of Messrs. W. &. C. K. Herrick, who have a handsome white marble building. This firm is largely engaged in the importation of foreign stationery. From John street we pass up Broadway to Chambers street, on the corner of which stands Stewart's Marble Palace, covering a space of 152 feet on Broadway and 100 on Chambers street.

On the site of the old Broadway Theatre, Judge Whiting has erected, at a cost of $200,000, a marble building, with 75 feet front on Broadway, by 175 feet deep.

At No. 340 Broadway is the ancient site of the famous Broadway Tabernacle, once known through the whole land as the great rendezvous of the various religious and benevolent institutions during the May anniversaries. The frontage on Broadway is 30 feet, and the depth 200 feet, with an extension on Worth street and Catharine lane of 100 feet square. This fine marble edifice is now the immense wholesale clothing house of Carter, Kirtland & Co. They occupy about an acre of floor room.

On the corner of Worth and Church streets, and occupying the whole block, is the massive stone building of Messrs. H. B. Claflin & Co.

Continuing up Broadway to the corner of Franklin street, we come to the International Hotel. The lofty saloon on the first floor, known as "Taylor's," contains an area of seven thousand five hundred feet. The view from the two grand entrances is magnificent.

On the corner of White street and Broadway stands one of the finest specimens of architecture of which our city can boast. The building is of white marble, and is

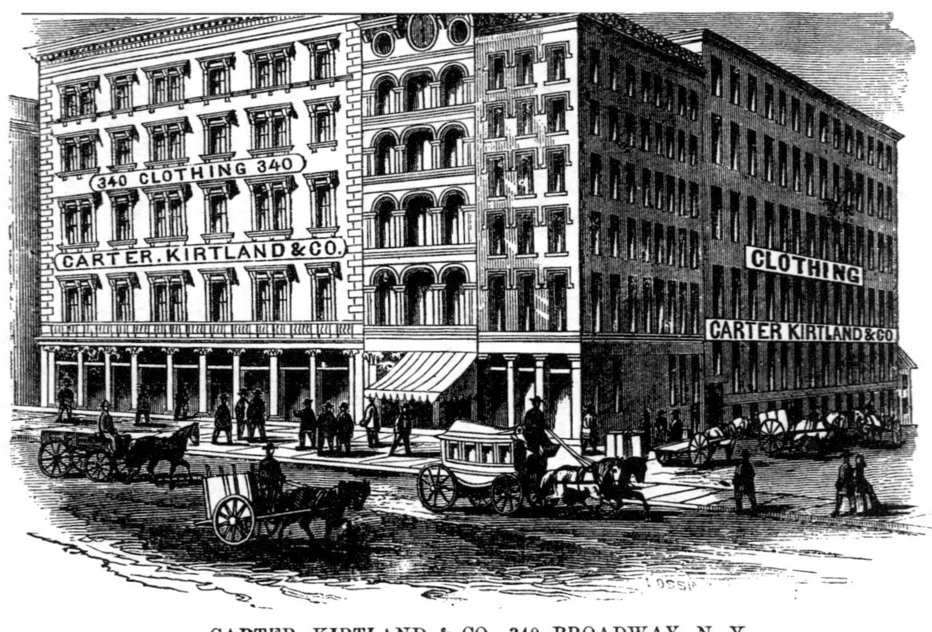

CARTER, KIRTLAND & CO., 340 BROADWAY, N. Y.

TIFFANY & Co.
[LATE]
TIFFANY, YOUNG & ELLIS
550

owned by Mr. Astor. Just above this, at No. 389 Broadway, Messrs. Fowler & Wells, the phrenologists, have their rooms.

The book-publishing establishment of D. Appleton & Co., 443 & 445 Broadway, attracts attention. They manufacture *Cartes de Visite* Albums, and have a large Bookbindery and Printing-office in Franklin St., and are extensively engaged in the manufacture of school books.

The attention is next arrested by the elegance of a building at the corner of Broadway and Grand street. It has a front of 100 feet on Broadway and 125 feet on Grand street. The whole structure is of highly ornamented white marble, and is occupied by Messrs. Lord & Taylor as a dry-goods store. On the lower corner, Messrs. Devlin & Co., the clothiers, have their store, whilst on the opposite corner Messrs. Brooks Brothers, also clothiers, occupy a fine brown-stone building. Messrs. Routledge, Warne & Routledge, the great London publishers, have their agency at 129 Grand street.

On the corner of Broome street and Broadway, is Messrs. E. V. Haughwout & Co.'s handsome iron building, and next door to them, at No. 494 Broadway, is the depot of the Elliot Arms Co., whilst opposite them is another iron building, in the Gothic style, occupied by the Grover & Baker Sewing Machine Co. Mr. Anthony has the building next to this for his Photographic Emporium. At No. 522 Broadway, opposite the St. Nicholas Hotel, is James Miller's book store. Here may be found, in addition to a large and well selected stock of both English and American books, everything in the stationery line that can be desired. Next door to Miller's, Messrs. Chase & Co. have their Ornamental Iron Works, and offer everything in that line from a wire railing to the most elegant statuary. Just above this, at 536 Broadway, is the Empire Sewing Machine Co., and directly opposite, at No. 537, the Dalton Knitting Machine Co.

At No. 552 Broadway is "Tiffany's." This was the first large establishment to remove "up town," but is now in the central portion of the metropolis. Their silverware and jewelry are mainly manufactured on the premises, and their retail trade alone amounts to over $1,000,000 per annum.

Opposite Tiffany's is the saloon known as "Upper Taylor's." Ball, Black & Co.'s new building is on the corner of Broadway and Prince street.

The next building which claims our attention is at No. 625 Broadway, and is known as the "Derby Art Gallery." On the ground floor is the show room of the Wheeler & Wilson Sewing Machine Co., which is one of the most beautiful of the Broadway stores.

We have now reached Astor Place, at the junction of which and Third Avenue is the Bible House. Passing to and continuing up Fourth Avenue, we arrive at Union Square, at the junction of which with the avenue stands Brown's Statue of Washington. It is a bronze equestrian figure, placed upon a plain granite pedestal. The statue is fourteen and a half feet, and the whole, including the pedestal, is twenty-nine feet high. It occupied the artist four years in its construction, and cost over $30,000. The statue is universally admired. The artist has, in a masterly manner, overcome the almost insurmountable difficulty of all equestrian statues, inasmuch as he has succeeded in making the interest of the horse subordinate to that of the rider. The majestic presence of Washington is the object first to catch and fix the beholder's gaze. The true proportions and fine attitude of the animal but enter into and complete the inspiring effect of the perfect statue. In the figure of Washington, we have the lofty-minded, imperious master of an else wilful steed, now curbed and subdued by a firm and practised hand; in the horse is seen only the proud bearer of a most noble burden. Before concluding, we would mention the bookstore of Messrs. Thomson Brothers, at No. 1107 Broadway. Citizens in their neighborhood, and sojourners at the Fifth Avenue and other hotels in their immediate vicinity, will always find the Messrs. Thomson's store well filled with books in every department of literature.

Nearly opposite their store is a beautiful granite shaft erected to the memory of General Worth. Its erection was celebrated by a public ceremonial.

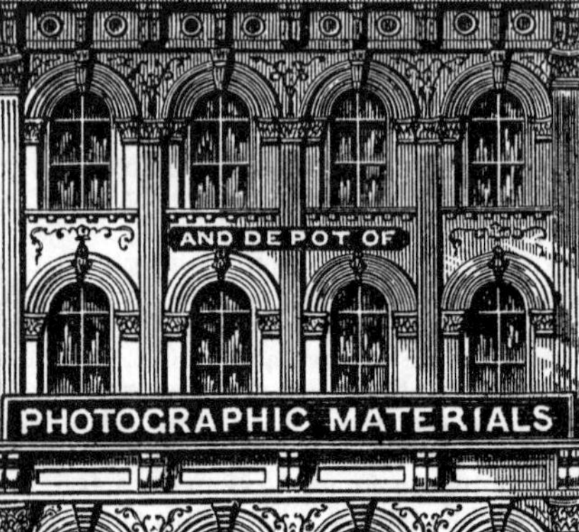
501
AMERICAN & FOREIGN
STEREOSCOPIC EMPORIUM
AND DEPOT OF
PHOTOGRAPHIC MATERIALS

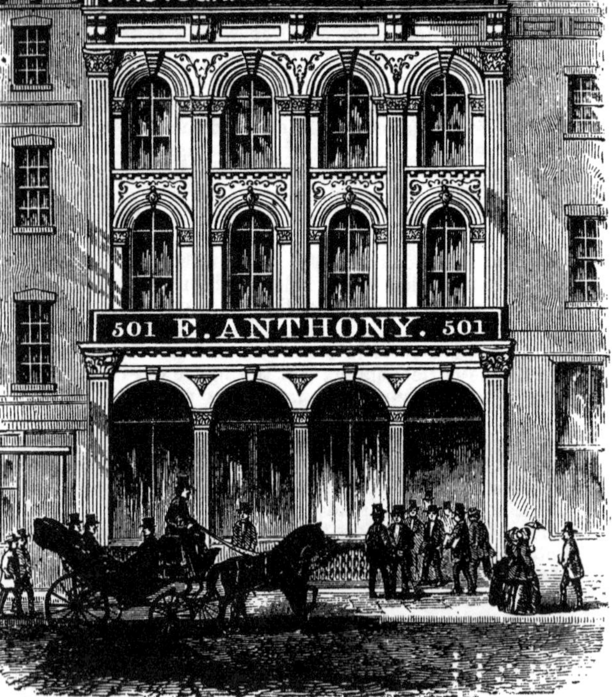
501 E. ANTHONY. 501

POST OFFICE.

Corner of Nassau and Liberty Streets.

Office Hours.—Daily at all hours, except Sundays. Sundays from 9 to 10 A. M., and from 12½ to 1½ P. M.

U. S. Mail Stations.—Open from 6.30 A. M. to 9.30 P. M.

A, 129 Spring street,	G, 1259 Broadway,
B, 439 Grand street,	H, Yorkville,
C, Fourth street, corner W. Twelfth street,	J, Harsenville,
D, Bible House,	K, Manhattanville,
E, 368 Eighth Avenue,	L, Harlem,
F, 408 Third Avenue,	M, Carmansville,
	N, Tubby Hook.

Rates of Postage.

No letter will be sent from this Office, to any place within the United States, *unless the postage is prepaid* by stamps.

Stamps and stamped envelopes can be procured at the office of sale, in the second story of the Post Office building; entrance at the east end of the Cedar street front, open from 9 A. M. to 3 P. M., at the first window from Cedar on Nassau street, and at all the stations.

The inland postage (which must be prepaid) upon single letters, is three cents; double letters twice, and treble letters, treble these rates.

Every letter or parcel not exceeding half an ounce in weight, shall be deemed a single letter, and every additional weight of half an ounce, or less, shall be charged with an additional single postage, prepaid by stamps.

City letters must be prepaid by stamps at the rate of two cents for each half ounce, or less, and two cents for each additional half ounce, whether delivered from the office or by the carriers.

Advertised letters are charged with one cent, in addition to the regular postage.

RATES OF POSTAGE.

No letters will be sent frem the Post Office to places within the United States, *unless the postage is prepaid* by stamps. Unpaid letters will be sent to the Dead Letter Office at Washington.

Stamps, in any quantity, can be procured at any of the "Stations" throughout the city.

The Inland Postage on letters for 3000 miles or under, is 3 cents; double letters twice this rate, etc.

Letters for California and Oregon, 3 cents.

Every letter not exceeding half an ounce in weight shall be deemed a single letter, and every additional weight of half an ounce, or less, shall be charged with an additional single postage.

City letters are subject to two cent postage.

Newspapers, magazines, and books must be prepaid.

BANKS.

The more prominent banks of New York include, the Bank of New York, corner of Wall and William streets, the Bank of America, the Mechanics' Bank, the Merchants' Bank, the Manhattan, the Bank of Commerce, Nassau Bank, &c. The Banks of New York are daily becoming more important in an architectural point of view.

The American Exchange Bank, 128 Broadway, corner of Liberty street, is a splendid building of Caen stone.

The Bank of Commerce, in Nassau street, facing the Post-Office, is one of the finest marble edifices in the city. Its capital is ten millions of dollars.

Duncan, Sherman & Co.'s Banking House is built of brown stone, and stands on the corner of Nassau and Pine streets; it cost $150,000. Adjoining this is another splendid establishment,—*The Continental Bank.*

The Bank of the Republic is situated at the corner of Broadway and Wall street; it is a noble edifice, built of brown stone; its entire cost is estimated at about $175,000. Its capital is $2,000,000.

The Metropolitan is also built of brown stone, and is located at the corner of Pine street and Broadway; its cost is stated at $160,000.

The Bank of the Commonwealth, 15 Nassau street, is a beautiful brown stone structure of elegant proportions.

The Bank of America is one of the old established banks, situated 46 Wall street. Its capital is $3,000,000.

On the corner of Wall and William streets, is another fine edifice, the *Bank of New York*; recently rebuilt with brick and brown stone facings; its capital is $2,000,000.

The Bank of North America, 44 Wall street, has a capital of $1,000,000.

Broadway Bank, corner of Broadway and Park Place, is a massive brown-stone building; its cost is stated at $127,000.

The Park Bank, on Beekman street, near Park Row, is a recent establishment, with a capital of $2,000,000.

The Phenix Bank, 45 Wall street.

The Shoe and Leather Bank, corner of Broadway and Chambers street, has a capital of $1,000,000.

The Union Bank, 34 Wall street, has a capital of $1,500,000.

The Importers and Traders Bank, 245 Broadway, has a capital of $1,500,000.

The Pacific Bank has recently erected a fine marble edifice in Broadway, adjoining Brooks' building, corner of Grand street.

The Manhattan Company, 40 Wall street, has a capital of $2,050,000.

The *Clearing House* is at 72 Broadway.

For a general list of the City Banks, the reader is referred to the New York Directory.

SAVINGS BANKS.

Among the excellent institutions of New York, may be mentioned the Savings Banks. The principal establishments are the following:

Bank for Savings, 67 Bleecker street, is a beautiful marble edifice, the most elegant and spacious of its class in the city.

Bowery Savings Bank, 130 Bowery, is a splendid brown stone building—one of the architectural ornaments of this portion of the city. We refer the reader to the annexed illustration of this edifice.

Broadway Savings Bank is on the corner of Park Place.

East River Savings Bank is situated 3 Chambers street.

The Irving, 96 Warren street.

The Greenwich, 73 Sixth Avenue.

The Emigrant Industrial, 51 Chambers street.

The Mechanics and Traders', 283 Bowery.

The Manhattan, 644 Broadway.

The Dry Dock, 663 Fourth street.

The Merchants' Clerks' Savings Bank, 516 Broadway.

Seaman's Bank for Savings, 78 Wall.

Sixpenny Savings Bank, Clinton Hall, Astor Place.

Croton Reservoir.

PUBLIC WORKS.

THE CROTON AQUEDUCT,

By which the city is supplied with pure water, is one of the most gigantic enterprises of the kind undertaken in any country. The distance which the water travels through this artificial channel, exclusive of the grand reservoir, is about forty miles. The Dam crosses the Croton River six miles from its mouth, and the whole distance from this dam, thirty-two miles, is one unbroken under-ground canal, formed of stone and brick. The great receiving reservoir is on York Hill, five miles from the City Hall; it can receive a depth of water to the extent of twenty feet, and is capable of containing 150,000,000 gallons. Two miles further on is the distributing reservoir, at Murray Hill. This reservoir is of solid masonry, built in the Egyptian style of architecture, with massive buttresses, hollow granite walls, &c. On the top of the walls is an inclosed promenade. It is three miles from the City Hall. The cost of this immense undertaking was over thirteen millions of dollars.

During the past year the works have been thoroughly examined and repaired from the Croton Dam to the receiving reservoir at a cost of $19,704. In connection with this a typographical survey of the valley of the Croton was effected, by which it appears that the ridge defining the waters above the point at which the Aqueduct begins, measures 101 miles. Within this circuit there are 31 lakes and ponds; and the aggregate area of waters including the tributaries is 352 square miles; which is equal to 96,034 gallons per square mile during the driest season. Yet large as this supply may appear, the resources of the Brooklyn water-works are nearly six times as great.

The construction of the New Reservoir, &c., now in progress, has already cost upwards of $300,000; these extensive works will, on their completion, entail a sum more than double that anount. By the report of the past year, the receipts by the authorities, including appropriations by the City Government, amounted to $1,764,112, the disbursements $1,291,826, leaving a balance of $472,286 for all contingencies, as well as the completion of these important improvements.

The New Reservoir is located at York hill, in the Central park, between Eighty-fifth and Ninety-seventh streets. The gate-houses, which are to cost $193,513, are to be built in the outer reservoir bank, and at the ends of the central bank of the new reservoir, the aqueduct will extend therefrom to about 50 feet east of the existing aqueduct, near the Ninth Avenue. The south gate-house will be located near Eighty-sixth street; 83 feet long, 40 feet wide, and 42 feet above the pavement of the bays, which are to be divided. The masonry will be very massive, and supported by buttresses four feet wide and sixteen feet high. The north gate-house will be 72 feet by 40, and correspond with the other so far a relates to distribution and waste-pipes, &c.

At the distance of about eight miles from the City Hall is

THE HIGH BRIDGE,

The most important structure connected with the Croton Aqueduct. It is thrown across the Harlem valley and river. It spans the whole width of the valley and river at a point where the latter is 620 feet wide, and the former a quarter of a mile. Eight arches, each with a span of 80 feet, compose this structure; and the elevation of the arches gives 100 feet clear of the river from their lower side. Besides these, there are several other arches rising from the ground, the span of which is somewhat more than half that of the first mentioned. The material employed throughout the whole of this

High Bridge.

imposing object is granite. The works cost $900,000. The water is led over this bridge, which is 1450 feet in extent, in iron pipes; and over all is a pathway, which, though wide enough for carriages, is available to pedestrians only. The fare by a carriage, allowing passengers to remain two or three hours at the bridge, is $5. It can be reached pleasantly and expeditiously by the Harlem Railroad (Depot 4th Avenue and 26th street), or in summer by the Third Avenue Railroad and steamboat from Harlem.

SHIP-BUILDING YARDS AND DRY DOCKS.

Of the numerous works in and around New York, the stranger must not fail to pay a visit to the *Ship-Building Yards* and *Dry Docks*, where gigantic steamers may be seen in every stage of progress, and all the most approved machinery connected with ship-building in active operation.

THE NOVELTY WORKS,

At the foot of Twelfth street, are of themselves a perfect marvel, and here the stranger may spend an hour with the greatest pleasure and profit in witnessing all the wonders of the steam-engine.

THE NAVAL DRY DOCK,

A stone structure, said to be the largest of the kind in the world, and a perfect monument of engineering skill, will also well repay the trouble of a visit. The dimensions of this gigantic dock are 400 feet in length by 120 in breadth at their base. The work took ten years in its construction; it cost $2,150,000.

THE SECTIONAL DOCK,

At the foot of Pike street, East River, is an object well worth visiting. The dock is constructed for the purpose of lifting vessels, by means of tanks filled with water. There is also another process of raising a vessel, by means of pulleys, worked by hydraulic power.

CLIPPER SHIPS, PACKETS, ETC.

The docks along the North River, from the Battery northward, and also especially along the East River, exhibit a complete forest of masts of the naval architecture of the city. Splendid packet-ships, clippers, and steamboats, of all descriptions and sizes, hem in the margins of these rivers. On the North River may be seen the stately ocean-steamers. These also are objects of interest to strangers, and they may inspect the elegant cabins of these splendid vessels on application.

FORTS AND FORTIFICATIONS.

The national defences of New York comprise the following: the strong fortifications of the Narrows—on the one side, *Forts Hamilton* and *La Fayette*, the latter having three tiers of guns, &c.; on the other side, *Forts Tompkins* and *Richmond*, situated on Staten Island heights. To protect the inner harbor, there are *Forts Columbus* and *Castle William*, on Governor's Island, and the works on Bedlow's and Ellis' Islands.

Castle William, measuring 600 feet in circumference, and 60 feet high, is a circular stone battery, with magazines, &c.

Fort Columbus, on the same island, connects with the former. Here are barracks and a corps of the United States troops.

Governor's Island, formerly known as Nut Island, from its formerly being covered with nut-trees, was, in colonial times, used by the English governors as

TAYLOR'S SALOON.

pleasure-grounds. The several fortifications here, may be easily seen, by taking a boat from Castle Garden, foot of the Battery. There are other fortifications for the defence of Long Island Sound, and also towards Sandy Hook.

PRINCIPAL RESTAURANT SALOONS.

These are *Taylor's Saloon*, the largest and most sumptuous in the city or country, No. 365 Broadway, corner of Franklin street.

Maillard's Saloon, in Broadway, adjoining St. Thomas' Church, corner of Houston street. There are two or three others on Broadway, in the neighborhood of Tenth and Twelfth streets.

The Refectories and Oyster Saloons are too numerous to detail, being accessible in almost every section of the city. The more important are the following:

Florence's, 609 Broadway.
Keefe's, 594 Broadway.
Pieris & Purcell's, 734 Broadway.
The Merchants' Restaurant, Astor House.
Delmonico's, corner of Broadway and Chambers st.
Geo. W. Browne's, 123 Water street.

The consumption of oysters in New York is immense; it having been computed that the daily consumption is valued at $15,000, and that some 1500 boats are constantly engaged to obtain the supply for this city alone.

PRINCIPAL HOTELS.

The Astor House, Broadway, near the City Hall Park
The Metropolitan, Broadway, corner of Prince street.
St. Nicholas, Broadway, corner of Spring street.
Prescott House, Broadway, corner of Spring street.
The Everett House, north side of Union Square.
La Farge House, Broadway, opposite Bond street.
New York Hotel, Broadway, cor. of Washington Place.
The Clarendon, cor. Fourth Avenue and Eighteenth st.
St. Denis, corner of Broadway and Eleventh street.
Union Place Hotel, Union Square.
Brevoort House, Fifth Avenue and Clinton Place.
St. Germain, Fifth Avenue and Twenty-second street.
The Julian, Washington Place, near Broadway.
The Fifth Avenue Hotel, corner of Fifth Avenue and Twenty-third street.

In addition to the above, there are numerous other hotels and houses, which may readily be ascertained.

NEW YORK MARKETS.

THE FULTON MARKET,

Built in 1821, at a cost of $220,000, is located on a block described by Fulton street on the south, Beekman on the north, Front on the west, and South street on the east.

WASHINGTON MARKET

Is on the western side of the city, on the North River, at the foot of Vesey street and Washington street. This market receives the produce from the West, as the Fulton does from the East district.

CATHARINE MARKET

Is smaller than the above, occupying a square between Cherry and South streets, East River. There are also

CHELSEA MARKET,

In the Ninth Avenue, near Eighteenth street;

JEFFERSON MARKET,

Corner of Greenwich and Sixth Avenues;

CLINTON MARKET,

Situate at the foot of Canal street, between the North River and Washington street; and

TOMPKINS MARKET,

Between Sixth and Seventh streets, Third Avenue.

There is yet another, more central, and on a larger scale, known as

CENTRE MARKET,

In Centre street, extending from Grand to Broome streets. This is a well-built and commodious place, adapted for the various departments of a public market. The building is substantial, built of brick, two stories high; the upper portion being used as armories and drill-rooms by military companies, &c.

THE OCEAN STEAMSHIPS.

The offices of the several lines of steamships are as follows:

Cunard Steamers.—E. Cunard, 4 Bowling Green.

U. S. Mail Steamship Co., for Aspinwall.—J. W. Raymond, 177 West street.

Glasgow Steamers.—R. Craig, 6 Bowling Green.

Charleston Steamers.—Spofford, Tileston & Co., 29 Broadway.

Pacific Mail Steamship Co.—88 Wall street.

The Liverpool and New York S. S. Co.—John G. Dale, 15 Broadway.

M. O. Roberts' Line to San Francisco and Oregon.—D. N. Carrington, 177 West street.

U. S. Mail Line for California via Panama.—D. B. Allen, No. 5 Bowling Green.

Steam to Hamburg, Havre, Southampton, and London.—C. B. Richard & Boas, 181 Broadway.

Mail Steamers to France direct.—The General Transatlantic Company's new line of first class side-wheel steamships between New York and Havre. George Mackenzie, Agent, No. 7 Broadway.

For Havana.—Spofford, Tileston & Co., 29 Broadway.

Advertisements of other lines are to be found either in the Directory, or in the columns of the New York *Herald.*

FOREIGN CONSULS.

Great Britain—E. M. Archibald, 17 Broadway.
France—Gauldree Boileau, 2 Bowling Green.
Spain—Juan Pico y Villanueva, 17 Broadway.
Mexico—Juan Navarro, 33 South street.
Russia—R. Ostensacken, 50 Exchange Place.

Interior view of the Office of the

MANHATTAN LIFE INSURANCE COMPANY,

Nos. 156 & 158 Broadway, New York.

Cash Capital & Accumulations - - - - - $2,250,000.

Enry Stokes, President. C. Y. Wemple, Secretary. J. L. Halsey, Ass't Secretary.

STEAMBOATS.

Albany (morning boat), Pier No. 40, N. R.
Albany (night boat), Pier No. 41, N. R.
Albany and Troy, Pier No. 15, N. R.
Astoria, Pier No. 24, E. R.
Boston (Fall River Line), Pier No. 3, N. R.
Boston (Stonington Line), Pier No. 18, N. R.
Boston (Norwich & Wor. Line), Pier No. 39, N. R.
Bergen Point, Pier No. 2, N. R.
Blackwell's Island, Foot of 26th Street, E. R.
Bridgeport, Pier No. 26, E. R.
Bull's Ferry, Pier No. 43, N. R.
Cold Spring, Pier No. 33, N. R.
Cornwall, Piers No. 33 & 35, N. R.
Catskill, Piers No. 34 & 40, N. R.
College Point, Pier No. 22, E. R.
Dobb's Ferry, Pier No. 33, N. R.
Elm Park, Pier No. 19, N. R.
Elizabeth, Pier No. 2, N. R.
Fort Lee, Pier No. 43, N. R.
Flushing, Pier No. 22, E. R.
Glen Cove, Pier No. 24, E. R.
Grassy Point, Pier No. 33, N. R.
Great Neck, Pier No. 24, E. R.
Greenwich, Pier No. 22, E. R.
Hastings, Piers No. 33 & 34, N. R.
Harlem, Pier No. 24 (Peck Slip), E. R.
Haverstraw, Pier No. 33, N. R.
Hartford, Pier No. 24 (Peck Slip), E. R.
Highlands (The), Pier No. 28, N.R.
Hudson, Pier No. 34, N. R.
Irvington, Pier No. 34, N. R.
Kingston, Pier No. 33, N. R.
Keyport, Piers No. 26 & 28, N. R.
Long Branch, Pier No. 28, N. R.
Mariner's Point, Pier No. 2, N. R.
Middletown Point, Pier No. 28, N. R.
Mott's Dock, Pier No. 24 (Peck Slip), E. R.
New Brighton, S. I., Pier No. 19, N. R.
New Haven, Pier No. 25, E. R.
Newark, Pier No. 20, N. R.
Newburgh, Pier No. 33, N. R.
Nyack, Piers No. 33 and 34, N. R.
Port Richmond, S. I., Pier No. 19, N. R.
Peekskill, Pier No. 33, N. R.
Perth Amboy, Pier No. 26, N. R.
Philadelphia, Atlantic Street, Brooklyn.
Port Monmouth, Pier No. 28, N. R.
Poughkeepsie, Piers No. 33 & 35, N. R.
Providence, Pier No. 3, N. R.
Rockland Lake, Pier No. 34, N. R.
Rossville, Pier No. 26, N. R.
Rondout, Pier No. 33, N. R.
Red Bank, Pier No. 28, N. R.
Sailor's Snug Harbor, S. I., Pier No. 19, N. R.
Sandy Hook, Pier No. 28, N. R.
Shrewsbury, Pier No. 28, N. R.
Sing Sing, Pier No. 33. N. R.
Staten Island (North Shore), Pier No. 19, N. R.
Staten Island, for Tompkinsville, Stapleton, and Vanderbilt's Landing, Pier No. 1 (foot of Whitehall street), E. R.
South Amboy, Pier No. 26, N. R.
Stamford, Pier No. 22, E. R.
Tarrytown, Piers No. 33 and 34, N. R.
Totten's, Pier No. 26, N. R.
Verplanck's, Pier No. 33, N. R.
Woodridge, Pier No. 26, N. R.
West Point, Pier No. 33, N. R.
Westchester, Pier No. 22, E. R.
West Park, Pier No. 33, N. R.
Yonkers, Piers No. 33 & 34, N. R.

TELEGRAPH OFFICES.

Principal Office of AMERICAN TELEGRAPH CO., No. 145 Broadway.

Sub-offices: Are located at the

Astor House, Broadway, bet. Vesey and Barclay streets.
Earle's Hotel, cor. Canal and Centre streets.
Metropolitan Hotel, Broadway, bet. Spring and Prince streets.
Lafarge House, 673 Broadway.
New York Hotel, 721 Broadway.
Fifth Avenue Hotel, cor. Broadway and 23d street.
Everett House, cor. Fourth Avenue and 17th street.
Merchants' Hotel, 41 Cortlandt street.
Westchester House, cor. Broome street and Bowery.
95 Eighth Avenue.
945 Broadway.
New Haven Railroad Depot, cor. 27th street and Fourth Avenue.
N. W. cor. 42d street and Sixth Avenue.
St. James Hotel, cor. Broadway and 26th street.
Allerton's, cor. Broadway and 40th street.
Merchants' Exchange, 50 and 52 Pine street.
Cor. Beaver and Pine streets.
Board of Brokers, William street.
Produce Exchange, cor. Whitehall and Pearl streets.
Washington Market Exchange, 190 Vesey street.
No. 83, Fish Market, Fulton Market.
Hudson River Railroad Depot, 68 Warren street.
Mercantile Agency, 293 Broadway.
Foot of Vestry street, N. R.
N. W. cor. Broadway and Canal street.
Dry Dock, cor. Avenue D and 10th street.
Hudson River Railroad Depot, 31st street, near Tenth Avenue.
S. E. cor. 130th street and Third Avenue, Harlem.
Cor. 86th street and Third Avenue.
Harlem Railroad Depot, cor. Fourth Avenue and 26th street.

OMNIBUSES AND RAIL-CARS.

The omnibus lines are 29 in number, comprising 671 vehicles, which average about 10 down and as many up trips daily. Besides these stages there are five lines of commodious city cars, drawn by horses or mules along rails laid on the streets. The fare is only 5 cents. They run as follows:

Harlem Co.'s City Cars—From Park Row to Centre street, through Centre to Grand, Grand to Bowery, up Bowery to Fourth Avenue and Twenty-seventh street.

Second Avenue Cars—From Peck Slip, through Pearl, Chatham, Bowery, Grand, and Allen streets, First Ave nue, East Twenty-third street and Second Avenue, to Harlem.

Third Avenue Railroad—Park Row, Bowery, Third Avenue, to Yorkville.

Sixth Avenue Railroad—Vesey, througn Church and Chambers streets, West Broadway, Canal, Varick, and Carmine streets, Sixth Avenue, to Fifty-ninth street.

Seventh Avenue Railroad—From corner of Broadway and Barclay street, through Church, Greene, University Place, Broadway, Forty-third street, and Seventh Avenue to Fifty-ninth street. There is also a branch starting-place from corner of Broadway and Broome street.

Eighth Avenue Railroad—Vesey, through Church, Chambers, West Broadway, Canal, Hudson streets, and Eighth Avenue, to West Fifty-ninth street.

Ninth Avenue Railroad—Barclay, corner of Church, through Church, Chambers, West Broadway, Canal, Greenwich, and Ninth Avenue, to Fifty-ninth street.

Central Park, North and East River Railroad—Eastern Division—From South Ferry, foot of Whitehall street, through Front, Water, and South streets, to Grand Street Ferry; thence through Grand, Mangin, Corlears and Houston streets, to Avenues D and A; thence through 14th street to First Avenue, and through First Avenue and 59th street to the Fifth Avenue entrance of the Central Park.

Central Park, North and East River Railroad—Western Division—From South Ferry, foot of Whitehall street, through Whitehall and State streets, Battery Place, West street, Tenth Avenue and 59th street, to Fifth Avenue entrance of Central Park.

Broadway and Grand Street Ferry Railroad—From junction of Broadway and Canal street, through New Canal street, East Broadway, and Grand street to Grand Street Ferry.

Broadway and Seventh Avenue Railroad—From junction of Broadway and Barclay street, through Barclay, Church, Greene, and Eighth streets, University Place, Broadway, Seventh Avenue, and 59th street.—Branch from junction of Broadway and Broome street, through Broome, Greene, Eighth streets, University Place, Broadway, Seventh Avenue, and 59th street. RETURN ROUTE—From corner of 59th street and Seventh Avenue, through Seventh Avenue, Broadway, University Place, Eighth street, Wooster street (Branch Road from Wooster through Broome street, to Broadway). Canal street, West Broadway, Barclay street, to Broadway.

Forty-second Street and Grand Street Ferry Railroad—Forty-second street and Eleventh Avenue, along Forty-second street to Tenth Avenue, through Tenth Avenue to Thirty-fourth street, Broadway, Twenty-third street, Fourth Avenue, Fourteenth street, Avenue A, Houston street, Cannon street, Grand street, to Grand Street Ferry. RETURN ROUTE—From Grand Street Ferry to Goerck street, through Goerck, Houston, and Second streets, Avenue A, Fourteenth street, Fourth Avenue, Twenty-third street, Broadway, Thirty-fourth street, Tenth Avenue to Forty-second Street Ferry.

East Broadway and Dry Dock Railroad—From junction of Park Row and Broadway, through Park Row, Chatham street, Chatham Square, East Broadway, Grand street, Goerck, Houston, to Avenue D, thence through Avenue D to Dry Dock. RETURN

Route—From Dry Dock, through Avenue D, Eighth, Lewis, Grand, East Broadway, Chatham Square, Chatham street, Park Row to Broadway.

Fourteenth Street and Fulton Ferry Railroad—From foot of Fourteenth street, North River, through Hudson, Bleecker, Crosby, Grand, Elm, Reade, Centre, Beekman, and South streets, to Fulton street; and return through Fulton, William, and Ann streets to Park Row, and thence to Fourteenth street along the route above mentioned.

For the several stage and omnibus routes throughout the city, see the New York Directory. Most of them have their routes designated on the outside of the vehicle. A large proportion of them pass up and down Broadway almost incessantly.

RAILROADS.

NEW YORK AND NEW HAVEN.

This is much frequented; the distance to New Haven is 76 miles; but the route is continued on to Springfield 63 miles further, and thence a distance of 100 miles more reaches Boston. The whole journey, which saves the passage on the Sound, is accomplished in about 8 hours. The depot is on the corner of Fourth Avenue and Twenty-seventh street. This road cost $4,233,000.

NEW YORK AND HARLEM.

The trains run on this road as far as Albany, stopping at intermediate places. As far as Williams' Bridge, which is 14 miles from the city, they run on the same track as the New Haven trains, afterwards they branch off. The Harlem tunnel, a quarter of a mile in length, is a wonderful excavation, being cut through solid granite;—while it is approached by a long deep cut of more than a mile in length. Cars leave the depot opposite the Astor House, every five minutes, for Twenty-seventh street, from half-past 7 A. M., to 8 P. M; and the night line every 20 minutes, from 8 to 12. Cars for Harlem, only, leave from the same place every hour throughout the day.

THE HUDSON RIVER.

The city depot of this road is at the junction of Chambers and Hudson streets, whence passengers are conveyed to the depot at Thirtieth street, corner of Tenth Avenue, for the locomotive. This road extends to Albany, and stops at the intermediate places. Its time-table varies, but can be had on application. This is considered the best-constructed road in the country; its cost, for 144 miles, is stated at $9,300,000.

NEW JERSEY RAILROAD.

For Washington, Baltimore, and Philadelphia, and intermediate places, leaves New York from foot of Cortlandt street, via Jersey City Ferry.

CENTRAL RAILROAD OF NEW JERSEY.

For Harrisburg, Reading, Pottsville, Mauch Chunk, and intermediate places, leaves Pier No. 2, N. R.

NORTHERN RAILROAD OF NEW JERSEY.

For Piermont and intermediate places, leaves New York from foot of Cortlandt street.

CAMDEN AND AMBOY RAILROAD.

For Philadelphia, via steamers to Amboy, leaves Pier No. 24, N. R.

MORRIS AND ESSEX RAILROAD.

For Hackettstown and intermediate places, leaves foot of Barclay street.

LONG ISLAND RAILROAD.

For Greenport and intermediate places, leaves James Slip, and foot of Thirty-fourth street, E. R.

CONEY ISLAND RAILROAD.

All Brooklyn horse-cars for Greenwood connect with this road. Depot, Thirty-sixth street, near Fifth Avenue, Brooklyn.

FLUSHING RAILROAD, L. I.

Leaves foot of 34th street, and James Slip, N. Y.

RARITAN AND DELAWARE BAY RAILROAD.

For Middletown, Red Bank, Long Branch, Tom's river, and intermediate places, leaves wharf foot of Murray street.

STATEN ISLAND RAILROAD.

For Tottenville and intermediate places, leaves New York from Pier No. 1, foot of Whitehall street, E. R.

FERRIES.

Brooklyn—Catherine Slip to Main street. From 4 A. M. to 10 P. M., every ten minutes; from 10 P. M. to 4 A. M., every twenty minutes.

Brooklyn—Foot Fulton to Fulton street. From 3 A. M. to 12 P. M., every ten minutes; from 12 to 3 A. M., every 15 minutes.

Brooklyn—Foot Jackson to Hudson Avenue. From 5 A. M. to 10 P. M., every fifteen minutes.

Brooklyn (E. D.)—Foot Roosevelt to South Seventh street. From 5½ A. M. to 9 P. M., every twenty-four minutes.

Brooklyn—Foot Wall to Montague street. From 5 A. M. to 9 P. M., every ten minutes; from 9 P. M. to midnight, every twenty minutes.

Brooklyn—Foot Whitehall to Atlantic street. From 5 A. M. to 9 P. M., every eight minutes; from 9 P. M. to 11 P. M., every fifteen minutes; from 11 P. M. to 5 A. M., every half hour.

Brooklyn (E. D.)—Foot Grand to Grand street, and to Division Avenue.

Brooklyn (E. D.)—Foot E. Houston to Grand street.

Bull's Ferry and Fort Lee—Pier No. 42 N. R.

Elizabethport—Pier No. 2 N. R.

Greenpoint—Foot Tenth and foot East Twenty-third. From 6 A. M. to 9 P. M., every fifteen minutes.

Hamilton Avenue—Foot Whitehall to Atlantic Dock. From 5 A. M. to 11 P. M., every twelve minutes; from 11 P. M. to 5 A. M., every half hour.

Hoboken—Foot Barclay. From 6 A. M. to 7¾ P. M., every fifteen minutes; from 7¾ P. M. to 12 P. M., every half hour; from 12 P. M. to 4 A. M., every hour; from 4 to 6 A. M., every half hour.

Hoboken—Foot Canal. From 5¼ A. M. to 9 P. M., every half hour.

Hoboken—Foot Christopher. From 6¼ A. M. to 7½ P. M., every half hour.

Hunter's Point—Foot East Thirty-fourth street. From 4½ A. M. to 12 P. M., every fifteen minutes. Fare three cents.

Hunter's Point—James Slip to Ferry street, every half hour.

Jersey City—Foot Cortlandt to Montgomery street. From 3 A. M. to 7½ P. M., every ten minutes; from 7½ P. M. to 12 P. M., every fifteen minutes; from 12 P. M. to 3 A. M., every thirty minutes.

Jersey City—Foot Desbrosses to Exchange Place. From 5 A. M. to 10 P. M., every fifteen minutes; from 10 P. M. to 5 A. M., every thirty minutes.

Mott Haven—Foot Peck Slip. Boats leave at 7, 8, 9.15, and 11 A. M., 1.15, 3.15, 4.15, 5.15, 6.15, and 7.15 P. M. From foot of Eighth street fifteen minutes later.

Pavonia—Foot Chambers, N. R., to Long Dock. From 1 A. M. to 7 P. M., every fifteen minutes; from 7 P. M. to 1 A. M., every half hour.

Staten Island—(New Brighton, Port Richmond, and Snug Harbor.)—Foot Whitehall. 5 trips daily.

Staten Island—(Quarantine, Stapleton, and Vanderbilt's Landing.)—Foot Whitehall. From 6 A. M. to 7 P. M., every hour. The 7 and 9 A. M. and 1, 4, and 6 P. M., connect with the trains of the Staten Island Railroad.

Weehawken—Foot West Forty-second. From 7 A. M. to 9 P. M., every fifteen minutes.

EXPRESSES AND DEPOTS.

Adams', East, South, and California, 59 Broadway.

American Express Company, North and West, Hudson, corner of Jay, and 124 Broadway.

Erie Railroad, Broadway, corner of Dey.

Harnden's, East and South, 65 Broadway.

Kinsley's, East and South, 72 Broadway.

National Express to Canada, 74 Broadway.

Harlem Railroad, Tryon Row, east of City Hall.

Hudson River Railroad, Chambers and Hudson street.

Long Island Railroad, Hunter's Point, Long Island.

New Jersey, 73 Courtland street.

Harnden's, Savannah and South, 65 Broadway.

LIST OF PIERS.

East River.

1, 2, foot Whitehall.
3, " Moore.
4, bet. Moore and Broad.
5, " Broad and Coenties slip.
6, 7, 8. Coenties slip.
9, 10, bet. Coenties and Old slips.
11, 12, Old slip.
13, b. Old sl. & Gouverneur's la.
14, foot Jones' lane.
15, 16, foot Wall.
17, foot Pine.
18, " Maiden lane.
19, " Fletcher.
20, 21, foot Burling slip.
22, " Fulton.
23, " Beekman.
24, bet. Beekman and Peck slip.
25, 26, foot Peck slip.
27, foot Dover.
28, bet. Dover and Roosevelt.
29, foot Roosevelt.
30, bet. Roosevelt and James.
31, 32, foot James' slip.
33, " Oliver.
34, 35, " Catharine.
36, 37, " Market.
38, (Z. Ring's) bet. Market and Pike slip.
39, 40, foot Pike.
41, (Sectional dock) bet. Pike and Rutgers.
42, 43, foot Rutgers.
44, " Jefferson.
45, " Clinton.
46, bet. Clinton and Montgomery
47, foot Montgomery.
48, not built.
49, foot Gouverneur's slip.
50, not built.
51, 52, foot Walnut.
53, 54, " Grand.
55, 56, " Broome.
57, " Delancey.
58, bet. Rivington and Stanton.

North River.

1, foot Battery place.
2, 3, bet. Battery place & Morris.
4, foot Morris.
5, 6, 6½. bet. Morris and Rector.
7, foot Rector.
8, 8½, bet. Rector and Carlisle.
9, foot Carlisle.
10, " Albany.
11, bet. Albany and Cedar.
12, foot Cedar.
13, foot Liberty.
14, bet. Liberty and Courtland.
15, 16, foot Courtland.
17, bet. Courtland and Dey.
18, foot Dey.
19, " Fulton.
20, bet. Fulton and Vesey.
21, foot Vesey.
22, bet. Vesey and Barclay.
23, 24, foot Barclay.

25, foot Robinson.
26, foot Murray.
27, " Warren.
28, " Chambers.
29, " Duane.
30, bet. Duane and Jay.
31, foot Jay.
32, " Harrison.
33, " Franklin.
34, " North Moore.
35, " Beach.
36, " Hubert.
37, " Vestry.
37½, " Desbrosses.
38, " Watts.
39, 40, foot Canal.
41, foot Spring.
42, bet. Spring and Charlton.
43, foot Charlton.
44, " King.
45, " Hamersley.
46, " Clarkson.
47, " Morton.
48, " Christopher.
49, " Amos.
50, " Charles.
51, " Perry.
52, " Hammond.
53, " Bank.
54, " Troy.

THE CITY OF BROOKLYN,

Being by far the largest and most important place adjacent to New York, claims more than a passing notice.

Brooklyn has, within the past few years, been characterized by the same degree of advancement as New York. Its present population is estimated at 200,000; while its numerous and elegant churches, public buildings, and stately private residences, render it equally conspicuous. It is a favorite place of residence by the New Yorkers, from its pure air, as well as its numerous trees, which line most of its streets, and impart to it a rural aspect. Fulton Avenue, Flatbush Avenue, and the intersecting great highways, are fine thoroughfares. Brooklyn, as to its name, is supposed to be derived from the Dutch, Breucklen (broken land). It was incorporated as a village in 1816. It has but few relics remaining. There is an old house, dated 1696, on the route to Gowanus, by the Fifth Avenne. It is known as the Cortelyou House.

The first European settler in this town is supposed to have been George Jansen de Rapelje, at the Waalnoght, or Waaloons Bay, during the Directorship of Peter Minuit, under the charter of the West India Company.

FORT GREENE,

An elevated plateau, northeast of the Brooklyn City Hall, was, during the Revolutionary war, the site of important fortifications. It has recently been laid out as a public park, and planted with trees. The view of the surrounding country from this elevation is exceedingly attractive.

THE CITY HALL

Faces the junction of Fulton and Court streets, and is distant from Fulton Ferry about one mile. It is a noble Ionic structure, built of Westchester marble, and admirably planned. It has a solid, substantial look. Its measurement is as follows: 162 feet in length by 102 in width; height 75 feet; to the top of the cupola the height is 153 feet. The cost of the Hall was about $200,000. The Park, which is inclosed with the building, is of a triangular form.

THE CITY ARMORY,

An elegant brick and brown stone structure, on the corner of Henry and Cranberry streets, occupies the site of the old Apprentices' Library, the corner stone of which was laid by Lafayette. The armory was finished, January, 1859. It measures 100 feet by 50—is four stories high, with basement. The three upper stories are occupied by the 13th, 14th, and 72d Regiments; the fourth being used as a general drill room. The cost was $14,300.

THE STATE ARSENAL

Is located on the corner of Portland Avenue and Auburn Place, opposite Fort Greene, on Washington Park. It is 200 feet by 60 in measurement, having 2 towers, and is 2 stories high. It incloses 14 lots of ground.

The 70th Regiment of Artillery have their quarters here. The cost was $40.000.

THE POST-OFFICE,

Formerly on Fulton street, is located in Montague street, in the building of the Mechanics' Bank, corner of Court street. The mail delivery between the General Post-Office of New York and Brooklyn, occurs two or three times every day.

THE ACADEMY OF MUSIC.

This is a noble edifice constructed of brick, and costing about $125,000. It is located on Montague near Court street, nearly opposite the City Post Office.

THE WATER-WORKS.

This great desideratum of Brooklyn has recently come into operation, and promises an abundant supply to its inhabitants of pure water. It has already been introduced into the streets and houses. The sources from which the supply is obtained is Rockville reservoir, and others adjacent to Hempstead, L. I. From thence it is conveyed by an open canal to Jamaica reservoir, through a conduit to Ridgewood reservoir, where it is forced up to an elevation sufficient to answer all purposes required. The water is pronounced equal, if not superior, in purity of taste to the Croton water.

THE KINGS COUNTY JAIL

Is situated in Raymond street, at the foot of Fort Greene. It is a dark, heavy-looking, castellated Gothic edifice in front, built of red sandstone, with Gothic windows at each side, and a large yard at the back.

THE UNITED STATES NAVY YARD,

At Brooklyn, well deserves the notice of visitors. It

is situated upon the south side of Wallabout Bay, in the northeast part of the city. It occupies about forty acres of ground, inclosed by a high wall. There are here two large ship-houses for vessels of the largest class, with workshops, and every requisite necessary for an extensive naval depot. A dry dock constructed here cost about one million of dollars.

The United States Naval Lyceum, an interesting place, also in the Navy Yard, is a literary institution, formed in 1833, by officers of the navy connected with the port. On the opposite side of the Wallabout, half a mile east of the Navy Yard, is the Marine Hospital, a fine building, erected on a commanding situation, and surrounded by upwards of thirty acres of well-cultivated ground. At the Wallabout were stationed the Jersey and other prison-ships of the English, during the Revolutionary war, in which it is said 11,500 American prisoners perished from the bad air, close confinement, and ill-treatment. In 1808, the bones of the sufferers, which had been washed out from the bank where they had been buried, were collected and deposited in thirteen coffins, inscribed with the names of the thirteen original States, and placed in a vault beneath a wooden building, erected for the purpose in Hudson Avenue, opposite Front street, near the Navy Yard.

It is estimated that the Navy Yard contains property to the amount of over $23,000,000.

THE ATLANTIC DOCK.

These extensive works are situated below the South Ferry, within what is called Red Hook Point, the outside pier extending some 3000 feet on the "Buttermilk Channel." They are owned by a Company, which was incorporated in 1840, with a capital of one million of dollars. The basin within the piers comprises about 42 acres, with a sufficient depth of water to receive ships of the largest size. The masonry of these granite works is very well worth visiting. The Hamilton Ferry, from the Battery, is the readiest approach to the Atlantic Dock.

THE LONG ISLAND COLLEGE HOSPITAL,

Henry street, near Pacific street, is a noble institution, liberally endowed, and occupying a spacious and elegant edifice, with grounds inclosed. It is sustained by the most eminent medical skill, and highly prosperous in its results, although but comparatively a recent institution.

THE FEMALE ORPHAN ASYLUM

Is situated in Congress street, and the

MALE ORPHAN ASYLUM,

In Bedford Avenue.

THE CITY HOSPITAL,

In Raymond street, near De Kalb Avenue, organized in 1845, took possession of its present edifice in 1852.

THE DISPENSARY FOR THE EYE AND EAR,

No. 109 Pineapple street, was established in 1850.

THE POLYTECHNIC INSTITUTE,

On Livingston street, between Court and Boerum streets, is a beautiful modern edifice, devoted to the education of young lads. It possesses a fine lecture-room, and is under the management of a regular faculty.

THE PACKER COLLEGIATE INSTITUTE,

For the instruction of young ladies, is situated in Joralemon street, between Court and Clinton streets. It is an elegant Gothic building of brick, and very spacious and elegant in its appointments. There is a large lec ture-room in the centre of the edifice, which is lighted by a long Gothic window.

There are in Brooklyn and its suburbs over 30 ward schools, some being of the largest dimensions, capable of accommodating 1500 to 1800 children, besides primary schools and schools for colored children.

BROOKLYN HOTELS.

THE PIERREPONT HOUSE,

In Montague Place, overlooking the Wall Street Ferry, is a very spacious and elegant establishment, possessing all the modern accessories of a first-class hotel, being adapted to every conceivable want.

THE MANSION HOUSE,

On Henry street, not far from the corner of Pierrepont street, is another of the large hotels, furnishing elegant accommodations for some 250 guests.

THE GLOBE HOTEL,

No. 244 Fulton street, is a conveniently located house for visitors. The Brooklyn cars pass it every five minutes. It is much frequented by officers of the navy

---

PUBLIC INSTITUTIONS.

THE BROOKLYN ATHENÆUM,

On the corner of Atlantic and Clinton streets, is a literary institution, containing a fine library, reading-room, lecture-room, &c. There is a Mercantile Library Association connected with it, on the plan of the New York society of that name. It is a handsome brick building, with stone facings. There is a good library connected with the Association.

THE LYCEUM,

Situate in Washington street, corner of Concord street, is a literary institution of repute. It contains a good library, designed for youth; also, a museum of natural history, lecture-room, &c.

THE BROOKLYN SAVINGS BANK,

On the junction of Concord and Fulton streets, has long been one of the architectural ornaments of this city. It is one of the most elegant, externally and internally, of the numerous elegant edifices of Brooklyn.

HALSEY BUILDINGS,

A splendid range of iron buildings, on Fulton street, facing the City Hall, present a fine specimen of architectural skill. The same remark will apply to the stately mansions that cluster along Montague street, Remsen street, and the vicinity of Wall Street Ferry, and several parts of South Brooklyn.

GREENWOOD CEMETERY.

(Office No. 30 Broadway.)

The situation of this cemetery is on Gowanus Heights, about two and a half miles from the South Ferry, whence visitors can easily be conveyed to the cemetery in an omnibus.

The cemetery is laid out in the most tastefully variegated manner, with fifteen miles of avenues, besides numerous paths. In its more elevated parts it commands beautiful and attractive views, such as the city of New York, with its bay and harbor, its islands and forts, and reaching away beyond all interjacent objects, it carries out the eye to the great ocean itself.

On the margin of "Sylvan Lake" stands the memorial of the fair, yet hapless girl of the forest "*Do-hum-me*," who so soon exchanged her bridal for her burial. Not far from this monument is the tomb of the friendless poet, McDonald Clarke, and near by, that of the young and beautiful votary of fashion, Miss Canda, whose sudden death caused such deep sympathy some years since. This magnificent tomb cost $10,000. Among the numerous costly monuments, ought to be named the Pilots' and the Firemen's columns.

This cemetery is 330 acres in extent, and is of undulating and varied character. Free admission is granted to the public on week days, by tickets obtainable from any undertaker, but on Sabbath this privilege is restricted to proprietors, their families, and persons who may be of their party. The principal avenue is named The Tour, and by keeping in this, strangers will secure the most favorable general view. A little careful attention, however, to the guide-boards in the grounds, will enable them, ere long, to thread their way through the more retired, but not less beautiful passages, within this solemn inclosure.

Some four or five miles eastward of Brooklyn are the Cemeteries of the Evergreens and Cypress Hills; they do not, however, compare with Greenwood for beauty of scenery or architectural adornment.

The vicinity of Brooklyn possesses many points of interest; we can but name some of them. *Williamsburgh*—which, were it not now incorporated with Brooklyn, would be considered a city of itself—*Flushing*, *Flatbush*, *Jamaica*, *Bath*, *Fort Hamilton*, *Coney Island*, *New Utrecht*, *Rockaway*, *&c.* Near *Guildford*, on a rocky peninsula, is the cave of the notorious pirate, Capt. Kidd; it is marked with his initials.

CHURCHES OF BROOKLYN.

In addition to numerous elegant stores and private mansions, that in many instances vie with those of the Fifth Avenue of New York, Brooklyn possesses about 80 churches. The most notable of these are

CHURCH OF THE HOLY TRINITY,

Corner of Clinton and Montague streets, is a splendid Gothic edifice, of brown stone, measuring, with the rectory adjoining, 160 feet; width, 80 feet. The windows are of richly-stained glass. That in the church, representing the scene of the Ascension, is especially noteworthy. This elegant edifice cost $100,000. The Rev. Dr. Littlejohn is the rector.

THE CHURCH OF THE PILGRIMS,

On the corner of Henry and Remsen streets, erected in 1845, is of stone, and built in the early Norman style. It is very spacious, measuring 135 feet by 80. In the main tower, about six feet from the ground, may be seen inserted a piece of the "Pilgrim Rock," from Plymouth. The lecture-room is at the rear of the church, and is very spacious. The cost of the building was about $50,000. Rev. Dr. Storrs, Jr., is the pastor.

GRACE CHURCH,

Situated in Hicks street, near Remsen street. It is built of brown stone, and presents a fair specimen of the florid Gothic. Its interior is very beautiful—length of the nave, 85 feet; width, 60 feet; and the chancel, 28 by 24 feet. There is an adjoining chapel, 60 by 22 feet. The cost of the church was $42,000.

CHURCH OF THE SAVIOUR

(Unitarian), on the corner of Pierrepont street and Monroe Place, is of red sandstone, in the pointed Gothic. It is an elaborately-decorated and symmetrical structure. The cost is estimated at $60,000. Rev. Dr. Putnam is the incumbent.

FIRST REFORMED DUTCH CHURCH,

At the rear of the City Hall, was erected in 1834. It measures 111 feet by 66; is of the Grecian order, and has a deep pediment, supported by eight massive Ionic columns, which impart to the edifice a fine effect. In the rear of the pulpit is an effectively-painted recess. The Rev. Dr. Dwight is the pastor.

PLYMOUTH CHURCH,

In Orange street, between Hicks and Henry streets, is perhaps the largest church in Brooklyn, and is yet found insufficient for the large concourse which attends the preaching of the Rev. Henry Ward Beecher, since the society contemplate the immediate erection of a yet more spacious building, on the Heights, near the Wall Street Ferry.

CHRIST CHURCH,

In Clinton street, is a Gothic building, measuring 100 feet by 60, with a tower 100 feet high. There is, in the rear of the church, a lecture-room. The cost was $28,000.

STRONG PLACE CHURCH,

South Brooklyn, is another fine Gothic edifice, built of stone, and much ornamented in the interior. The Rev. Dr. Taylor is the pastor.

THE FIRST PRESBYTERIAN CHURCH,

In Henry street, near Clarke, is a massive-looking structure; lecture-rooms, &c., attached.

THE DUTCH REFORMED CHURCH,

In Pierrepont street, is a remarkable structure, and well

worth visiting. Its interior is exceedingly beautiful, and said to have been modelled after the earliest Christian church, built by the mother of Constantine. Its elaborate, yet chaste decorations present a rich effect. The Rev Dr. Bethune, till recently, was the pastor.

ST. ANN'S CHURCH,

Corner of Sands street and Washington, is one of the early churches of Brooklyn; and although of a modest exterior, has a plot of green sward surrounding it which is very inviting to the eye.

THE METHODIST CHURCH,

In Clinton street, near Atlantic, is a rough-hewn stone edifice, of the Norman style; over the principal entrance there is a large circular window. The interior is neat and attractive in its arrangement.

There are numerous other religious edifices, which proves that it is no misnomer which has been applied to Brooklyn—"the City of Churches."

CITY RAILROADS.

The *Brooklyn City Railroads* take the following routes, starting from the Fulton Ferry: one line runs through Fulton street, up Fulton Avenue, terminating at East New York, about 7 miles from the City Hall; another passes through Sands street to Williamsburgh; a third line goes up Fulton street, Myrtle Avenue, to Division Avenue; a fourth passes up Fulton street, through Court street, to Greenwood Cemetery, and the fifth from South Ferry, through Atlantic Avenue to Bedford.

PLEASURE EXCURSIONS.

The environs of New York abound in picturesque retreats for the lover of rural beauty. Not only are abundant facilities rendered available to the pleasure tourist, in the multiplicity of modes of conveyance by land or by water, but the geographical position of the metropolis places within the circuit of a few miles almost every variety of beautiful scenery, as well as villages, towns, and localities of historic interest. For a cool sea-breeze and pleasing aquatic excursion, the trip by the steamer for Shrewsbury and Long Branch, or Coney Island, will be found full of interest. Boats for the former leave foot of Robinson street, North River, and Peck Slip, East River, daily; for the latter the boat starts from the foot of Battery Place.

STATEN ISLAND

Is a place of much attraction as a summer resort, and the boats make the trip every hour, from Whitehall dock, near the Battery, The scenery is exceedingly fine, and the drives to the Telegraph station, Stapleton, Richmond, New Brighton, with their clusters of beautiful villas and country seats, are full of attraction.

HOBOKEN,

On the New Jersey shore, is Hoboken, with its Elysian fields and pleasure grounds, the bold bluffs of Weehawken, the Sybil's cave, and the memorable spot of the duel between Col. Burr and General Hamilton. The boats for Hoboken leave every half-hour from Canal street, Barclay street, and Christopher street ferries.

THROG'S POINT

Is another pleasing excursion. Sixteen miles from the city. It is the termination, at Long Island Sound, of Throg's, or rather Throgmorton's Neck. From this headland, which divides the East River from the Sound, a very splendid view is obtained. Fort Schuyler, on the point, and Pelham Bridge, may be embraced in this excursion.

ASTORIA.

A third excursion may take for its terminus the thriving village of *Astoria*, six miles to the northeast of New York. The academy, botanic gardens, &c., are worthy of notice; but its most interesting feature is the singular whirlpool in its neighborhood, denominated Helle Gat—"Hell Gate"—by the Dutch.

CROTON DAM.

A visit to the great Croton Aqueduct is one of the most interesting expeditions, as well as the easiest, that could be devised. The village of Croton is about 35 miles from the city, which is reached best by the Hudson River Railroad. The famous *Dam* pertaining to the works is well worthy of a visit. The lake, measuring 5 miles, covers an area of 400 acres; it is formed by a dam 250 feet long, and 38 feet wide at the base, allowing a discharge of 60 million gallons of water daily. Cars leave the Chambers-street depot, at the junction of West Broadway, every hour.

DAVID'S ISLAND,

Which may be reached by taking the New Haven cars to New Rochelle, and thence by stage to the ferry, is now occupied as a hospital for sick and wounded soldiers, and is admirably arranged under the superintendence of Dr. Simmons of the army. It is well worth a visit.

THE ENVIRONS OF THE CITY.

FLUSHING.

A pleasant trip to the entrance of Long Island Sound, brings one to Flushing, a remarkably rural and picturesque town, with extensive botanic gardens, nurseries, and numerous elegant residences. It is a chosen suburban retreat of the New Yorkers. The Flushing boat leaves, twice a day, the dock adjoining the Fulton Ferry.

FORT HAMILTON,

An attractive place on the southwestern shore of Long Island, about five miles from the city; and

CONEY ISLAND,

A short distance beyond, forming a part of Gravesend Township, is a sea-girt barren sand-heap, but commands a splendid view of the ocean, and is a place of much resort by bathers. Cars from Brooklyn, and boats from pier No. 1 North River, New York, leave daily for these places.

JAMAICA,

Which is easy of access by the L. I. Railroad, South Ferry, which leaves three or four times a day, is an interesting old rural town, and is the highway of communication to Hempstead, Greenpoint, Rockaway, and Montauk: the last named, on the extremity of the island, affords a magnificent view of the broad ocean, which there skirts the horizon in almost every direction. There is a remnant of pure Indians still living on this eastern extremity of the coast.

ROCKAWAY BEACH

Is another fashionable watering-place; there is a splendid hotel here, and every accommodation for the comfort of the valetudinarian. Turning again to the shores of New Jersey on the west, we find no less inviting attractions.

JERSEY CITY,

With its prodigious Depot of the Philadelphia and other trains, its noble Ferry Depot, and its numerous factories, streets of busy merchants, &c., first greet us. This city is the starting point of several important railroad trains, which convey the tourist at almost any hour to the several places we shall briefly specify: namely—

PATERSON,

A large manufacturing village, with its picturesque Falls of the Passaic—one of the most romantic cascades that are to be seen. The water is not of great volume, but its precipitous leap over rocky precipices, gives to the scene a beautiful effect.

ELIZABETH CITY

Is another place of interest, not only from its being one of the oldest settlements in the State (1664), but also on account of its handsome buildings, and beautifully arranged streets, which are garnished with the richest foliage.

NEWARK,

One of the most important manufacturing cities of the State, is fast becoming a great centre of activity in all the useful arts. Being a convenient halting-place for the Philadelphia trains, this city has increased with wonderful rapidity during a few years. It abounds with magnificent churches, and is considered in all respects a model city for its municipal and civil order. Newark's first settlement is ascribed to an ancient date, 1666, by a colony from New England. Many other adjacent places might be mentioned, as worthy of note, such as

NEW BRUNSWICK,

Also an incorporated city, with its celebrated Princeton College, &c.,

PERTH AMBOY,

So named from its originally having been chartered to the Earl of Perth in 1683, is a neat and picturesque watering-place.

DISTANCES IN THE CITY.

FROM BATTERY.	FROM EXCHANGE.	FROM CITY HALL.	TO
¼ mile.			Rector street.
½	¼ mile.		Fulton.
¾	½		City Hall.
1	¾	¼ mile.	Leonard.
1¼	1	½	Canal.
1½	1¼	¾	Spring.
1¾	1½	1	Houston.
2	1¾	1¼	Fourth.
2¼	2	1½	Ninth.
2½	2¼	1¾	Fourteenth.
2¾	2½	2	Nineteenth.
3	2¾	2¼	Twenty-fourth.
3¼	3	2½	Twenty-ninth.
3½	3¼	2¾	Thirty-fourth.
3¾	3½	3	Thirty-eighth.
4	3¾	3¼	Forty-fourth.
4¼	4	3½	Forty-ninth.
4½	4¼	3¾	Fifty-fourth.
4¾	4½	4	Fifty-eighth.
5	4¾	4¼	Sixty-third.
5¼	5	4½	Sixty-eighth.
5½	5¼	4¾	Seventy-third.
5¾	5½	5	Seventy-eighth.
6	5¾	5¼	Eighty-third.
6¼	6	5½	Eighty-eighth.
6½	6¼	5¾	Ninety-third.
6¾	6½	6	Ninety-seventh.
7	6¾	6¼	One Hundred and Second.
7¼	7	6½	One Hundred and Seventh.
7½	7¼	6¾	One Hundred and Twelfth.
7¾	7½	7	One Hundred and Seventeenth.
8	7¾	7¼	One Hundred and Twenty-first.
8¼	8	7½	One Hundred and Twenty-sixth.

STREETS AND AVENUES.

The length of the blocks between First and One Hundred and Twenty-first streets, vary from 181 to 211 feet 11 inches.

Those between the Avenues (which run at right angles to the streets), vary from 405 to 920 feet.

The Avenues are all 100 feet wide, excepting Lexington and Madison, which are 75, and Fourth Avenue, above Thirty-fourth street, which is 140 feet wide.

The numerical streets are all 60 feet wide, excepting Fourteenth, Twenty-third, Thirty-fourth, Forty-second, and eleven others, north of these, which are 100 feet wide.

THE HUDSON RIVER.

The tour of the noble Hudson is of such especial attraction and interest to travellers, that we deem it fitting to devote a page or two to its description. This magnificent river has been appropriately styled the Rhine of America, on account of its bold and picturesque scenery, which presents every variety of the beautiful in nature. On the western shores may be seen the long line of its natural ramparts—the palisades; on the opposite side, its magnificent slopes and towering heights crowned with numerous elegant country mansions. Adjacent to West Point are the colossal Highlands—those grand old mountain-peaks that rear themselves into the blue sky; and farther up, on either side, are the numerous towns and hamlets that gem the margin of this renowned historic river. Not alone for physical beauty is the Hudson celebrated; it is full of historic and legendary lore. Its waters are vocal with the hallowed reminiscences of our Revolutionary struggle; and all along its shores linger memo ries of heroic deeds of our forefathers. Its rocks and valleys are chronicled with the blood of the martyrs and heroes of freedom.

What though no cloister gray, nor ivied column,
  Along these cliffs their sombre ruins rear;
What though no frowning tower, nor temple solemn,
  Of tyrants tell of superstition here;
There's not a verdant glade, nor mountain hoary,
But treasures up the memory of freedom's story.

While nature has been thus lavish in her decorations of this noble river, art has fitted up for the accommodation of the lover of the picturesque, those costly and elegant aquatic palaces—the steamboats, which have been long, and so justly, the pride of New York. Harriet Martineau mentions, in her book on America, that if she were a New Yorker, she would sleep three nights out of the week, during summer time, on board the Hudson river steamers. These floating palaces are the frequent resort, not only of the stranger, but also of the denizens of the city, who seek the refreshing free air and enchanting scenery afforded by such an excursion. As the vessel leaves the dock, we first pass the Elysian fields of Hoboken, Weehawken bluff, and Bergen heights, on the west, and the long line of the city wharves and factories on the east. A little farther onward rises Fort Lee, a rocky bluff which commences the palisades, and which extend some twenty-five miles up the river, and then strike inland. The palisade range are of trap-rock, and resemble the Giant's Causeway, in Ireland. The island of Manhattan, on which New York is situated, is of primitive granite, while the opposite shore is of the tertiary formation. Among other prominent buildings which garnish the edge of the island, may be seen the *Orphan* and the *Lunatic Asylums*, also numerous cottages and villas. The town of *Manhattanville* is next visible, beautifully embosomed in a valley, being surrounded with hills. Here the celebrated naturalist Audubon resided. *Carmansville*, about nine miles from the city proper, is clustered with neat rural residences, and is a favorite resort of New Yorkers, as a suburban retreat. Near this spot is the *High Bridge*, which carries the Croton aqueduct across the Harlem river. One mile farther is the bold, rocky height, known as *Fort Washington*, memorable in our Revolutionary annals. It was the scene of a sanguinary en counter with the invading army, in which the British lost eight hundred men, and we some two thousand prisoners. The next object of interest is *Spuyten Duyvel Creek*, the origin of which name is humorously described in Knickerbocker's History of New York. This stream, which flows into the Harlem river, forms the northern boundary of the island of Manhattan. The next town we meet, some sixteen miles from the city of New York, is *Yonkers*, a beautiful and picturesque spot, and one of great resort as a rural retreat. It is full of elegant villas and pretty cottages. Near the town are *Fordham*, with its Roman Catholic College, and *Tetard's Hill*, noted in Revolutionary history. *Hastings* is the next place of note. Here the palisades begin to recede from the river. *Dobb's Ferry*, an important spot in Revolutionary times, is situate on the western shore. On the opposite side of the river is the residence of Washington Irving—*Sunnyside.* This beautiful, antique villa is scarcely visible from the water, being enveloped with the thick foliage which surrounds it. It is styled *Wolfert's Roost*, in the "Sketch Book." The pleasure-grounds of Mr. Irving's residence are laid out with excellent taste, and the picturesque beauty of the place, as well as the world-wide fame of the author, render it the great attraction of tourists from all parts of the world. We notice a little further up, *Piermont*, on the west, the starting point of the Erie Railroad. About three miles beyond is *Tappan* village, with its spreading bay. Tappan is celebrated as being the head-quarters of Washington during the war of Independence, and also of being the place of Major André's execution, in 1780. *Tarrytown*, distant twenty-six miles from New York, is famed as the place of the capture of André, by

Paulding and his compatriots. The spot is indicated by a monument, erected about half a mile northward of the town. About two miles distant is "Sleepy Hollow," the scene of Ichabod Crane's adventure with the "Galloping Hessian," so amusingly described by Irving, in his Legend of Sleepy Hollow. The scene is in excellent keeping with the story—a death-like stillness reigns here, which is only disturbed by the low murmuring of the mill-stream. Every person who wants a fitting book to amuse him on his trip up the Hudson, should make *Irving's Sketch Book* his *companion du voyage.*

Sing-Sing, 32 miles distant, is now in view, and from its elevated position presents an imposing aspect. Here is the State Prison, 444 feet in length, built of marble dug from the neighboring quarries. Opposite Sing-Sing, across Tappan Bay, which at this point is widest, is *Verdritege's Hook*, a bold headland, on the summit of which is a lake, the source of the Hackensack river. *Croton Village* is 8 miles farther, with its river which supplies New York with its water. *The Croton Aqueduct* and *Reservoir* are objects of great interest. These splendid works cost about $14,000,000. The fountain reservoir is 40 miles from New York. The dam built at this place is 250 feet long, 70 wide at the base. On the western side is *Haverstraw*, and 3 miles above it *Stony Point*, the site of the historic fort of that name. Directly opposite is *Verplank's Point*, also interesting for its historic associations. *Peekskill* is a romantic and picturesque place, and abounds with beautiful residences. On the opposite shore is *Caldwell's Landing*, which is at the base of the Dunderburg, or thunder-mountain. Passing on, we next see the small but picturesque *Buttermilk Falls*, about 200 feet in descent. *West Point*, distant 50 miles, is the next place of attraction, and affords, doubtless, the most magnificent series of beautiful scenery in America. It is surrounded with the Highlands, and commands from its great elevation an extensive and ever-varying succession of picturesque aspects. The Military Academy is one of the noble institutions of the Government, and an object of great interest. The beautiful grounds attached are laid out with taste and elegance, and are much resorted to by visitors. The Hotel is an establishment of the first class, and excellent in all its appointments. The view from the observatory of this hotel is very extensive and imposing. Near the steamboat landing is seen the rock from which the chain was stretched across the river during the Revolutionary war. Almost every spot of ground at West Point has historic interest. Fort Clinton stood where the Academy is now. Fort Putnam, and most others, are now in ruins. Passing through the magnificent mountain range we reach *Cold Spring* and *Undercliff*, the residence of Gen. G. P. Morris. On the opposite side of the river, but invisible from the water, is *Idlewild*, the residence of N. P. Willis. The next prominent village is *Fishkill*, 60 miles distant, and here the mountain scenery is in all its grandeur; but we soon pass to a different style of the picturesque. *Newburg*, on the opposite shore, noted as the head-quarters of Washington, is a large town, built on a steep acclivity. The next place of note is *Poughkeepsie*, also built on an eminence, and eminently picturesque. There are numerous minor villages, along either shore, all the way on to *Albany*, the capital of the State; but as the pleasure tourist may not possibly wish to extend his trip to 150 miles, we shall here respectfully part company.

SUPPLEMENTAL HINTS.

Persons who, for the first time, visit a great city like that we have already briefly described, doubtless fancy themselves in a very Babel of excitement and confusion; and would gladly accept the services of some good cicerone, or guide, who could conduct them through its perplexing mazes, pointing out what there is to see, and how to see it. No city of the New World is so truly cosmopolitan in its character as New York; consequently it presents an almost endless variety of objects of interest for the visitor. It is difficult to describe its many-hued aspects, for it is, in fact, an epitome of the civilized world; and the physical as well as the moral aspects of the city present a like complicated character.

As the tour of the entire city would be a too arduous performance for a pedestrian, we would advise the visitor to limit his perambulations to Broadway, from the Bowling Green to Union Square. Along this great promenade he will see enough to engage his attention for one day. Here are to be seen a long succession of splendid marble stores, churches, theatres, etc. Throughout the whole length of this great artery of the city, are to be seen the ebb and flow of a ceaseless tide of human beings, of every class and order; the belles and beaux of fashion, the busy devotees of toil, and the hapless ones who have not the will to work; men who seek their illicit gains at the gaming-table, and who practise upon the unwary at mock auctions.

Commencing, then, our journey up Broadway from the Bowling Green, the first noteworthy object we observe is the hotel at the southwestern corner, formerly *Kennedy House*, described in the chapter on Historical Localities. Passing several rows of stone buildings, including *Adam's Express* office, we reach *Trinity*

Church, the metropolitan church, which, being open to visitors, should certainly claim our attention. Not only should the interior be seen, but we ought to ascend the lofty steeple to view the magnificent panorama it affords of the city and its suburbs. We ought also to take a saunter among the venerable memorials of the sainted dead, not forgetting the recently erected Gothic monument to the memory of the martyrs of our Revolutionary struggle. Leaving Trinity Church and looking down Wall street, immediately opposite, we catch a partial glimpse of the *United States Treasury* on the north side; and further down on the opposite side of the street, the *Custom house*, a huge, colossal granite structure, where importers do chiefly congregate. On the corner of Wall street and Broadway stands the elegant edifice of the Bank of the Republic, and at the junction of the next (Pine) street we see the Metropolitan Bank; also, a superb marble building, occupied by Insurance Offices, &c. We now need Argus' hundred eyes to look about us; for not only is it a perilous thing to attempt to pass over from one side of the street to the other from the incessant crowding of all sorts of vehicles, but we are every moment in danger of being jostled or pushed aside by the still greater crowds of pedestrians, all eagerly in pursuit of something. There are some further demands made upon us, also, by the shops which invite our curiosity by their novel and motley contents. We now reach the junction of Fulton street and Old St. Paul's Church, with its sacred inclosure, containing the tall monument of the patriot Emmett, and the tombs of other celebrated characters. Facing this time-honored sanctuary, and in strange contrast with it, we notice *Barnum's Museum*, which is crowded to excess with curiosities of all descriptions, but too numerous to mention. We pass on a few paces to the *Astor House*, the earliest establishment of its class, and still one of the most elegant of the larger hotels of the city. Here we see the *Park*, *City Hall*, the *Times Office*, the *Tribune building*, and old *Tammany Hall*, the head-quarters of the stern democracy. In the intersecting streets to the west, between the Astor House and Stewart's, we catch a glimpse of long lines of splendid marble buildings, which give an imposing indication of the mercantile opulence of the city. At the rear of the City Hall we notice, at the junction of Chambers street and Broadway, *Stewart's Dry-Goods Palace*, occupying an entire block on Broadway. This is the great emporium of costly shawls, satins, silks, brocades, &c. It is now, however, devoted to the wholesale trade, the retail being removed to Stewart's new palace on Broadway, between Ninth and Tenth streets.

Passing up Broadway we soon approach the old-fashioned *Hospital*, with its noble avenue of trees. The more recent additions to this establishment are to be seen extending on the street to the south. The magnificent marble structure opposite the Hospital is that of *McNamee & Co.*, another well-known dry-goods establishment. On the site of the late *Broadway Theatre* are some elegant new stores occupied by wholesale merchants. As we continue our up-town progress, we pass numerous other large buildings, including *Taylor's* sumptuous saloon, and presently we cross *Canal* street, which, until within a quarter of a century, formed the boundary limits of the city in this direction. Pursuing our tour toward *Grand* street, we notice on the west side the white marble structure occupied by the *Appletons*, booksellers, and above on the east side *Brooks'* brown stone building, and opposite to it *Lord & Taylor's* dry-goods establishment, one of the most conspicuous architectural ornaments of Broadway. The next street *en route* we pass is *Broome* street, at the corner of which is the elegant iron building of Haughwout & Co., a museum of superb statuettes, articles of *vertu*, &c. Farther on, on the west side, stands the celebrated *St. Nicholas* hotel, extending to Spring street. On the opposite corner is the *Prescott House*, with its

BROADWAY, AS SEEN FROM DR. CHAPIN'S CHURCH.

gorgeous decorations. The next important edifices we meet are *Dr. Chapin's Church*, with the Dusseldorf Gallery, and *Tiffany & Co's* magnificent establishment. A little farther on is the fine marble building of *Ball, Black & Co.*, and at the corner of Houston street is the old *St. Thomas' Church*, opposite to which is the great *Metropolitan Hotel* and *Niblo's Theatre.* Still farther up we cross Bleecker street and reach the *Lafarge House*, another superb hotel, and the *Winter Garden*, (late Burton's). *The Olympic Theatre* is on the eastern side, a little below. Broadway is proverbial for its incessant changes and improvements, but from *Canal Street to Grace Church* these mutations will be found most conspicuous to persons who have not visited the city for the past few years. *Grace Church* is regarded as the culminating glory of Broadway. Its delicate spire and richly chiselled exterior, as well as its superb though too gaudy interior, render it the object of universal observation.

A short distance farther up brings us to *Union Square*, with its inclosed pleasure-grounds and fountain. On either side are elegant mansions and hotels. At the north the *Everett House* meets our gaze; on the west *Dr. Cheever's Church*, and on the southeast corner is the *Equestrian Statue of Washington* with the *Union Square Hotel*, &c. From this point we catch a glimpse of the *Academy of Music*, on the corner of 14th street and Irving Place. Our peregrinations are not yet completed. The Fourth Avenue, which extends northward from the east side of Union Square, leads us to numerous objects of interest, such as *Dr. Bellow's Church*, a singular specimen of medieval architecture, built with layers of different colored brick, and cased with stone facings. *Dr. Coxe's* (Calvary) *Church*, with two pointed towers, built in the cathedral style; and *St. Paul's* (Methodist) *Church*, of pure marble, are adjacent. We have before indicated that the Fifth Avenue is the head-quarters of New York aristocracy, and abounds with the sumptuous residences of our merchant princes. This splendid avenue extends northward to the *Croton Aqueduct*, and the better mode of entering upon this expedition, is to hire a carriage and take a leisurely drive through this grand avenue up to the Aqueduct and the *Central Park*. It would be well to adopt the same plan with the eastern part of the city, to the Shipping-Yards, Dry-Docks, &c. Brooklyn, which is virtually a part of New York, is by no means to be omitted, for it is replete with interest, and is easily accessible by means of the several ferries. The churches of both cities are fully detailed, for these form a characteristic feature, and well deserve the notice of the tourist. The several larger hotels are also specified, and those on a less expensive scale, which abound in New York, can be ascertained without difficulty. The visitor should not forget the many beautiful environs of the city.

APPENDIX.

THE METROPOLITAN POLICE.

The recently organized Department of Protective and Detective Police of New York and Brooklyn, is considered eminently effective and successful. The heads of the Department appointed by the State Legislature, comprise a Board of Commissioners, J. A. Kennedy, General Superintendent, and George W. Embree, Chief Clerk, etc. By the last quarterly report, it appears that the Police force of the City of New York consists of twenty-six Captains, one hundred and five Sergeants, forty-two Roundsmen, sixty Detailments, one thousand two hundred and fifty Patrolmen, and fifty-six Doormen.

The Police Telegraph has become an important auxiliary in the prevention and detection of crime, and also is a great convenience to the public. By this medium, several hundred lost children have been restored to their homes, and many thousand instances of criminals brought to justice.

By the statistics submitted to the Board of Supervisors, it is shown that the most fertile source of crime is the dramshop. There are in this city seven thousand seven hundred and seventy-nine places where intoxicating liquors are sold at retail.

The Police force of Brooklyn is organized on the same plan, and numbers in all two hundred and forty-eight.

The city of New York is divided into twenty-six Districts, the station-houses of which are situated as follows:

POLICE STATIONS.

COMMISSIONERS' OFFICE—300 Mulberry Street.

First Patrol District—Station House, at Franklin Market.
Second Patrol District—Station House, 49 Beekman street.
Third Patrol District—Station House, 79 Warren street.
Fourth Patrol District—Station House, 9 Oak street.
Fifth Patrol District—Station House, 49 Leonard street.
Sixth Patrol District—Station House, 9 Franklin street.
Seventh Patrol District—Station House, foot of Gouverneur st.
Eighth Patrol District—Station House, Prince, cor. Wooster st.
Ninth Patrol District—Station House, 94 Charles street.
Tenth Patrol District—Station House, Essex Market.
Eleventh Patrol District—Station House, Union Market.
Twelfth Patrol District—Station House, 126th st., n. Third Av.
Thirteenth Patrol District—Station House, Attorney, cor. Delancey street.
Fourteenth Patrol District—Station House, 53 Spring street.
Fifteenth Patrol District—Station House, 220 Mercer street.
Sixteenth Patrol District—Station House, W. Twentieth street, between Seventh and Eighth Avenues.
Seventeenth Patrol District—Station House, First Avenue, cor. Fifth street.
Eighteenth Patrol District—Station House, E. Twenty-second street, near Second Avenue.
Nineteenth Patrol District—Station House, East Fifty-ninth street, near Third Avenue.
Twentieth Patrol District—Station House, 212 W. Thirty-fifth street.
Twenty-first Patrol District—Station House, E. Twenty-ninth street, near Fourth Avenue.
Twenty-second Patrol District—Station House, Eighth Avenue, near W. Forty-eighth street.
Twenty-third Patrol District—Station House, State, cor. Whitehall street.

HOW TO LEAVE NEW YORK.

For Philadelphia, via New Jersey R. R. Depot at Jersey City. Proceed to 171 Broadway, thence to the foot of Cortlandt street, and cross the Ferry.

For Philadelphia, via Camden and Amboy R. R. From Pier No. 24 North River. Proceed to No. 227 Broadway, and west through Barclay street to the River.

For Boston, via Stonington and Providence. From Pier No. 18, North River. Proceed to No. 171 Broadway, and west through Cortlandt street to the River.

For Boston, via Fall River and Newport. From Pier No. 3, North River. Proceed to No. 1 Broadway, and west through Battery Place to the River.

For Boston, via Norwich and Worcester. From foot of Vestry street. Proceed to No. 417 Broadway, and thence through Canal street to the River.

For Boston, via New Haven R. R. Depot, 27th street and 4th Avenue. Take a 4th Avenue car, which starts from Astor House, or a Broadway and 4th Avenue stage, north to 27th street.

For Albany, via Hudson River R. R. Depot, Warren street and College Place. Proceed to 260 Broadway, west in Warren street to College Place.

For Albany, via Harlem R. R. Depot, 26th street cor. 4th Avenue. Take a 4th Avenue car, which starts from Astor House, or a Broadway and 4th Avenue stage, north to 26th street.

For Albany, via People's Line Steamboats. From foot of Canal street. Proceed in Broadway to No. 417, and west through Canal street to the River.

For Buffalo or Dunkirk, via N. Y. & Erie R. R. Depot, foot of Duane street. Proceed in Broadway to No. 303, and west in Duane street to the River.

For New Haven, by Steamboat. From Peck Slip. Proceed to No. 208 Broadway, and east in Fulton street to the River; thence northeast two blocks.

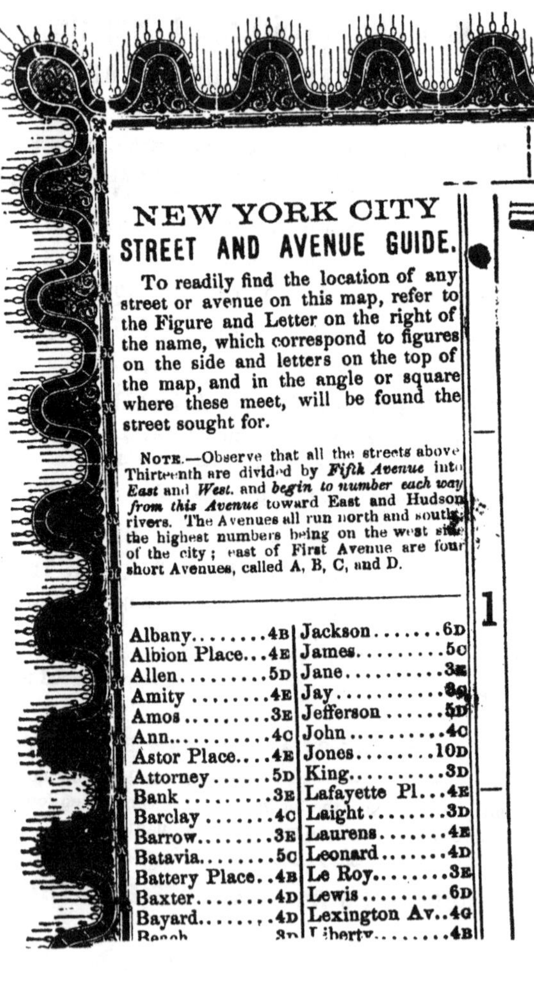

NEW YORK CITY

STREET AND AVENUE GUIDE.

To readily find the location of any street or avenue on this map, refer to the Figure and Letter on the right of the name, which correspond to figures on the side and letters on the top of the map, and in the angle or square where these meet, will be found the street sought for.

Note.—Observe that all the streets above Thirteenth are divided by ***Fifth Avenue*** into ***East*** and ***West***, and ***begin to number each way from this Avenue*** toward East and Hudson rivers. The Avenues all run north and south, the highest numbers being on the west side of the city; east of First Avenue are four short Avenues, called A, B, C, and D.

1

Albany........4B
Albion Place...4E
Allen.........5D
Amity 4E
Amos 3E
Ann...........4C
Astor Place....4E
Attorney......5D
Bank 3E
Barclay 4C
Barrow........3E
Batavia........5C
Battery Place..4B
Baxter........4D
Bayard.......4D
Beach.........3D

Jackson.......6D
James.........5C
Jane..........3E
Jay...........3C
Jefferson......5D
John..........4C
Jones........10D
King..........3D
Lafayette Pl...4E
Laight........3D
Laurens.......4E
Leonard.......4D
Le Roy........3E
Lewis.........6D
Lexington Av..4G
Liberty.......4B

INDEX.

	PAGE
Academy of Music	64
——— Design	59
Artists' Studios	58
Astor Library	48
——— House	66
Asylum for Aged Females	42
American Institute	55
——— Geographical Society	55
Apprentices' Library	52
Athenæum Club	81
Atlantic Docks	110
Barnum's Museum	64
Banks of New York	86
Battery, The	27
Benevolent Societies	43
Bible House, The	57
Bowery Theatre, New	64
Bowling Green, The	27
Brooklyn, City of	107
——— City Hall	108
——— Armory and Arsenal	108
——— Post-Office	109
——— Water Works	109
——— Navy Yard	109
——— Atlantic Dock	110
——— Hospital	111
——— Schools and Institutes	111
——— Hotels	112
——— Cemeteries	113
——— Churches	115
——— Railroads	117
Blind, Institution for the	44
Bloomingdale Asylum	40
Brevoort House	69
Bryant's Minstrels	65

PAGE

Carriage Fares.......... 65
Carmen.......... 65
Central Park.......... 29
City Hall of New York.......... 35
Children's Hospital, &c.......... 42
Churches of New York.......... 71
Clarendon, The.......... 68
Clubs, The.......... 81
College of Physicians.......... 43
Columbia College.......... 55
Consuls, Foreign.......... 96
Cooper Institute.......... 49
Croton Aqueduct.......... 89
——— Dam.......... 119
Custom House, The.......... 36

Deaf and Dumb Institute.......... 44
Demilt Dispensary.......... 42
Depots, Railroad.......... 102
Dispensaries of New York.......... 42
Distances in the City.......... 122
Dry Dock, The.......... 91

Education, Board of.......... 56
Egyptian Museum.......... 64
Environs of New York.......... 120
Everett House.......... 69
Excursions.......... 118
Expresses.......... 105

Ferries.......... 104
Fifth Avenue, The.......... 131
——— Hotel.......... 70
Fort Greene.......... 108
Forts and Fortifications.......... 92
Free Academy, The.......... 50

German Theatre.......... 64
Geographical Society.......... 55
Gramercy Park.......... 29
Greenwood Cemetery.......... 113

Hackney-Coaches.......... 90
Hall of Records.......... 88
Halls of Justice.......... 88
Harlem Railroad.......... 102

PAGE
High Bridge 90
Home for the Friendless 45
Hospital, New York 41
—— St. Luke's 42
Hotels of New York 46 94
House of Industry 45
—— and School of Industry 45
How to leave New York 135
Hudson River Railroad 102
Hudson River, The 123

Industry, House of 45
Insane, Asylum for 40
Institution for Deaf and Dumb 44
—— Blind 44
International Hotel 66

Jews' Hospital 41

Lafarge House, The 69
Leake and Watts' Asylum 43
Libraries of New York 51
Literary and Scientific Institutions 48
Long Island College Hospital 111
Lyceum of Natural History 52

Madison Square 29
Magdalen Asylum 43
Markets of New York 94
Marine Societies 47
Masons' Lodges 46
Medical College, The 43
—— School of the University 55
Merchants' Exchange 86
Mercantile Library Association 51
Metropolitan Police 138
—— Hotel 66

National Academy of Design 59
Navy Yard, The 109
New Haven Railroad 102
—— Bible House 57
New York Clubs 81
—— Theatres, &c 63
—— Picture Galleries 58
—— Public Buildings 35

PAGE
New York Parks.......... 27
—— Historical Localities.......... 5
—— Retrospect of.......... 18
—— General View of.......... 20
—— as it is.......... 25
—— Orphan Asylum.......... 40
—— Hospital.......... 41
—— Dispensaries.......... 42
—— Medical Colleges.......... 43
—— Libraries.......... 51
—— University and Colleges.......... 55
—— Bible House.......... 57
—— Scientific Institutions.......... 49
—— Newspapers.......... 60
—— Hotels.......... 66
—— Restaurants, &c.......... 93
—— Banks.......... 86
—— Churches.......... 71
Novelty Works, The.......... 42

Odd Fellows' Hall.......... 46
Olympic Theatre.......... 63
Omnibuses and Cars.......... 99
Orphan Asylum.......... 40
—— Leake and Watts.......... 48

Parks and Squares.......... 27
Packet Ships and Steamers.......... 92
People's Bathing Establishment.......... 48
Picture Galleries.......... 58
Piers, The.......... 106
Places of Amusement.......... 62
Porterage Rates.......... 90
Post Office, The..........85, 86
Prescott House.......... 68
Private Residences.......... 80
Public and Ward Schools.......... 56
—— Buildings.......... 85
—— Works.......... 89

Rail-cars and Omnibuses.......... 99
Railroads.......... 102
Randall's Island.......... 89
Restaurants and Saloons.......... 93

Sailors' Snug Harbor.......... 47

PAGE
Sailors' Benevolent Societies.............................. 47
Saloons, &c.. 93
St. John's Park.. 28
St. Luke's Hospital...................................... 42
St. Nicholas Hotel....................................... 67
St. Denis Hotel.. 69
Savings Banks.. 88
Schools, Public.. 56
Scientific Institutions.................................. 49
Sectional Dock... 91
Seminaries, Theological.................................. 58
Ships and Clippers....................................... 92
Society for Relief of Widows............................. 45
Societies, Benevolent.................................... 43
Stores, Notable.. 82
Statues, Public.. 84
Steamships... 95
Supplemental Hints....................................... 128

Telegraph Stations....................................... 98
Theatres... 63
Theological Institutions................................. 58
—— Union Seminary.. 58
—— Episcopal Seminary..................................... 58
Times Office... 60
Tompkins Square.. 29

Union Square... 28
United States Assay Office............................... 37
—— District Court.. 35
University of New York................................... 55
—— Medical School.. 43
Wallack's Theatre.. 63
Ward Schools... 56
Ward's Island.. 39
Washington Square.. 28

www.ingramcontent.com/pod-product-compliance
Lightning Source LLC
LaVergne TN
LVHW010742120826
845150LV00009B/1405

* 9 7 8 1 4 2 5 5 1 7 2 7 4 *